Quantum
Sobriety

Jo De Rosa

Foreword by Keith Wilson,
the Chocolate Shaman

Graphic Design and Layout: Dzined Ltd

DISCLAIMER:
We are not a medical facility and if you are physically dependent to a substance we advise you receive medical treatment for this before undertaking any of our programmes. Your physical dependency must be addressed first. Once your body is ready, then it is time to retrain your mind and create a new healthful reality.

Readers of this publication agree that neither Jo De Rosa nor her publisher will be held responsible or liable for damages that may be alleged or resulting directly or indirectly from the reading of this publication.

Acknowledgements

Thanks to everyone who has played a part in my journey thus far, allowing me to find my way to freedom. Sometimes the teachers showed themselves in an obvious way, while others provided painful lessons that I could never have understood had I not experienced them directly.

Special thanks to Dominic, my fabulous husband. What a journey of faith we have been on! Wow, I am so proud of what we have achieved together, and individually, and I thank you from the bottom of my heart for seeing the raw and true me.

Keith and Barbara have been a constant support, as have my other teachers. Grateful thanks to Samye Ling monastery where I get my yearly mental health check in the form of the annual Nyungney practice and Holy Isle where I wrote this book in its entirety over two separate retreats.

The Quantum Sobriety community blows my mind every day; how so many are stepping up into their power and shaking off their conditioned past is truly inspirational. What the group is achieving today was beyond my wildest dreams when I began to write this book in 2015 and I am so proud of every single member who has sat on their cushion and done one of the Quantum Sobriety meditations. Some stayed for a few months whilst others remain in the community, becoming senior members or 'Quantum Guides'. This book is for you all.

There are many more who had a hand in this, and you know who you are. I thank you all for supporting and loving me as I serve the world in the best way I can.

Dedication

For the Quantum Sobriety global community, and
everyone who opens the door to their heart and
welcomes freedom into their lives.

Contents

Foreword

My friend Jo has written a book for you out of her own journey and extensive experience. I am blessed to have played a part in her fun. So here you are on an adventure called addiction. Have you handled your sensitivity that no one understands, in this way? Have you handled the tension and stress of being different and having no place to put that difference where it is accepted, in this way? Have you felt powerless to control your life and filled, or hidden, that emptiness, with something, in this way? Have all those people, especially you, talked you out of who you are, and you ease the loss, in this way? Have you sensed a world of higher consciousness, and this was the only door you could find? Have you just needed a vacation from yourself or the world? Have you reached the place where you are tired of being beat up on, judged, told you have a problem that you are powerless against… rather than a solution that isn't working for you? Ready to finish telling that to yourself?

In a culture that teaches people to be disconnected from themselves and others, have you attempted to ease that emptiness with something to fill, dull, or cover your awareness of the missing connection… instead of recovering what is natural to us all… understanding that your pain is an indication of what an exceptional person you must be? Passionate, powerful, aware people who have been taught they aren't enough as they are, often attempt to deal with this cultural insanity as best they can.

This book is about first finding within what you don't see outside… as nothing, and no one else, can give it to you until you love yourself enough to give it to yourself. And then it's everywhere. Do you need to stop condemning yourself for a wonderfully strong desire to feel good? As you become more of who you really are, your impulses will change. The passion and power of your desire for something better will become a blessing to yourself, others, and this world. One big energy will become another. What if you designed it this way? We can say that you grew up in belief systems insisting you lack something, can't have it, or it isn't there… and one journey of finding something to fill that void, or hide it, is called addiction.

We could say that finding that positive connection is like becoming addicted to something that is much more joyous and of service to humanity. In this book are tools to help you do that. Along with the tools, this book will help with the courage to go wherever you need to go to discover and go beyond what you have been trying to find, or to cover up, through your addictive adventure. Let your addiction be a declaration that you haven't given up… as so many have. Time to take that determination to another level. And have more fun.

Blessings,
Keith, the Chocolate Shaman
November 2017, on the shores of Lake Atitlan, Guatemala.

Introduction

The saying 'we are creatures of habit' couldn't be truer. We absolutely are. It is how we are wired up, and ultimately what this book is about: how to unlearn unhelpful habits and create new positive, supportive and empowering ones.

We wake up at the same time with our alarm, have a hot cup of something, make breakfast, have a shower, brush our teeth and get dressed. We then get in our car and make the same journey to work, see the same people, do the same job, come home and have dinner, watch some TV, go to bed and then wake up the next morning and do exactly the same again.

For most habits are helpful, they keep us on track and on time, but for some of us that is not the case. We become addicted to substances, behaviours and certain emotions with catastrophic consequences. We forfeit our health, family, marriage, finances and internal equilibrium, and if that sounds like you then I have written this book for you.

Over the years I've been addicted to many different things, desperately craving the very thing that was destroying me. And I could see it happening, but seemed powerless to the lure of the instant gratification that I knew it would give.

This book is the story of/about how I overcame all of my addictions, to not only come out the other side alive, but to find freedom in my sobriety.

I have created a whole new reality for myself, one where I never wish I could have just one glass of wine with dinner or just one line of coke or one cigarette. That part of me that hankered over substances has GONE; I'm simply not that person anymore, and there is absolutely no effort on my part to be here. I am totally free.

The journey, however, has been a rough one! There didn't seem to be any support network that resonated for me through my own recovery, so I began my own unique journey out of addiction 20 years ago, finally finding complete freedom in 2012. What that means is that 16 years of effort to work this all out comes to you today in one book! And I so wish someone had written this before and given it to me 20 years ago, as I would have been free so much quicker…

Forming A Bridge

What is contained in this book is based on scientific proof, *and how to put it into practice,* of how meditation can change your life and, therefore, your brain. BUT! I have no academic qualifications: no degree, no A levels, just two C-Grade GCSE's. I bring you this technical information from the non-academic side of the fence rather than from a scientist's point of view, in a way that it is easy to understand, absorb and instantly put into practice.

You see, I knew instinctively from an early age that it was going to be my life experiences themselves that would be my greatest teachers. And so I eagerly left school at 16 for full-time employment, began the daily two-hour commute into London and fully immersed myself into being an 'adult'.

It was such a relief to shake off study, exams and the education system, and I grew up quickly, with my first mortgage at 20 years old. The story from there is colourful and one to which I will refer throughout this book, but the point I'd like to make right from the start is that I am as normal as normal can be.

I became a Buddhist 12 years ago and have been meditating for longer than that, so I have a lot of hours on the cushion and insight into the nature of my own mind. So with one foot in the mystical world of Buddhism and the knowledge of and participation in sacred teachings, and the other in the experience of every day first world living, my task is to translate the message so that everyone can understand it.

And I believe that I have been called to do this because I am a street-wise Buddhist! I've partied all night in a field; commuted into central London for over a decade; struggled with my relationships, addictions, work and money. I am you. I am the girl next door. *I speak your language.*

What I find so exciting is that YOU the reader can discover this path too. There is no reason why not, in fact anyone and everyone can do this, it is not limited to scientists, Buddhists or academics.

However I am going to turn your world upside down and inside out, and challenge how you view yourself, the world and what is even possible.

What do you believe? Do dreams come true? Can you create the life that you have always longed for? What is possible?

Quantum Sobriety is not just about the removal of drugs and alcohol from your life, although that was my own personal journey, but rather a whole system of eliminating all destructive behaviour, be it anger, food, fear, sugar, smoking or judgement, along with the more recognisable addictions of alcohol, drugs, gambling, self-harm and sex.

Anyone who regularly experiences *any* of these things is out of balance, and Quantum Sobriety addresses all of these issues by:

- going to the underlying cause
- pulling out the root
- planting new more positive seeds
- believing, with the backup of science, that ANYTHING is possible
- coming into alignment with your own personal truth.

This is the amazing world of Quantum Sobriety.

Before we get started, though, I like everyone going through any of my programmes to fill in this questionnaire. It is where we are starting from and before you read another word I request that you go and pick up a pencil or pen and jot down your answers NOW.

With these questions it is important to answer immediately without too much thought and with no hesitation. It is imperative that we know where you are starting from.

EXERCISE ONE: <u>Beginning Questionnaire</u>

Please answer these questions honestly and fully from the heart.

- How do you feel *right now* about yourself in 3 words:
    1. ....
    2. ....
    3. ....

- How stressed do you feel *right now* on a scale of 1 to 10?
  1 being not stressed and 10 being very stressed:

  ....

- How happy do you feel *right now* on a scale of 1 to 10?
  1 being not happy and 10 being very happy:

  ....

- How would you describe your addiction in one sentence:

  ....

  ....

- How is your addiction affecting your work life?:

  ....

  ....

- How is your addiction affecting your home life?:

....

....

- List here the problems that your addiction creates:
    1. ....
    2. ....
    3. ....
    4. ....
    5. ....
    6. ....

- What are three changes that you would like to make for you to be happier and healthier:
    1. ....
    2. ....
    3. ....

- How would you like to feel?:
    1. ....
    2. ....
    3. ....

So the only question now is, are you ready to find out about your Quantum Superpower and come into alignment with who you really are?

Part One:

All Worlds Collide

The Discovery Of A Superpower

Can you imagine how amazing it would be if we had superpowers? If we were able to have everything that we want, find happiness and enjoy the best of health? What if I were to tell you that it was possible? Would you believe me?

To obtain my superpower I had to first go through a load of 'life' before I could access it. For some this struggle appears to be essential, while others seem to be born with an automatic connection to the power.

My journey has been the whole of my life; I can see that the past 45 years have been a preparation for what is now. There were no mistakes; everything that I have been through was necessary. Every tear, all the come-downs, arguments and feelings of craving, sadness, rejection and fear. I had to go through it all to lay down the foundations for who I am today.

I have been hungrily learning about how to have less struggle throughout the last few decades until these layers of understanding and insight have finally cemented into a programme which can be shared, taught and learnt.

So it doesn't matter where I find you as you read this. You may be in a really good place relationship-wise, job-wise, and health-wise. Or you may be on the floor, up to your neck in addiction, debt and unhappiness, *and don't worry I've been there and know what that feels like*.

The wonderful news is that wherever you are now is perfect. You have access to this information, and from TODAY life will change. You are going to take back control, and the crazy thing is that you do that by relinquishing control: one of life's cheeky paradoxes.

You are going to learn to let go of all the things that hold you back and stop you from being *who you really are* under the layer of life. Perhaps right now it feels so heavy it is crushing you? Well it doesn't have to be like that, and I am going to show you the door to a new reality.

The Battle To Be Better

Although I can see that my whole life has been a journey, it started to get interesting in my twenties when I decided that I wanted to stop smoking, and couldn't. A battle of addiction commenced which panned across three decades, gave me many sleepless nights, caused me to throw up countless times from toxic overload to the point where I felt that I was perhaps going mad.

Because even back then something had awakened within me and I realised that I wanted BETTER for myself, and the struggle to pull myself out of the state in which I found myself had begun.

So I fought nicotine addiction from the age of around 23 (although I started smoking at 15) until I was 34 when I smoked my final cigarette. At this time I was also partying hard and taking recreational drugs every weekend and sometimes during the week also. I hung my party shoes up at 34 as well as kicking the nicotine habit, although at this time I really didn't understand my addictive tendency and swapped drugs for alcohol, and a whole new level of addiction was born.

By this time I was already teaching yoga and meditation

and had been living what felt like a double life. The 'old' Jo pulled me back towards the hedonistic life of sensual pleasure and what I called at the time 'fun'. But the switch had already been flicked and I had become serious about the pursuit of being the best I possibly could be.

Living on Koh Samui, Thailand between April 2000 and June 2006 was an example of living two lives: I lived above my retail shop in a lovely village on the north of the island where I also frequented many of the hippest bars, and this was very much my comfort zone. I'd take ecstasy, cocaine, and magic mushrooms along with smoking many cigarettes, sometimes staying up for two or three days at a time partying.

This usually happened over the weekend and I would emerge again on a Monday morning and drive my moped across the island to where I was teaching yoga at a detox retreat. I feigned a different persona as I walked through the door with my students assuming I was some sort of health guru, I don't think any of them ever realised what I'd been doing a few hours before, and they would have been shocked and appalled had they known, I'm sure.

Sometimes my two worlds bumped into each other as I sat outside my shop smoking cigarettes and drinking beer, and I'd spot some of my students walking along the street looking for me. Many a time I'd throw my cigarette in the street, run inside and brush my teeth, and then once again apply the 'healthy Jo' mask.

For a time I thought I had it all, the best of both worlds: smashed out of my head dancing to hardcore house at the weekend, and tranquil and serene on weekdays. Of course there was no way I could maintain such a façade. I had to choose what I wanted; go back to who

I'd been, or let go of the past and move forwards to become the enhanced version of myself that I sensed lurking deep inside.

And I knew which it was going to be, but that journey was not an easy one. The drugs were fun even though the come-downs were awful, and I couldn't even visit my usual hangouts and be around drugs without doing them, which meant life was about to become very different.

At this point I felt that life was like a huge pendulum: partying and swaying all the way over to the right, and then yoga-ing all week and swaying all the way over to the opposite left side. It seemed that there were literally just a few hours in the balanced place in between.

However this pendulum example doesn't demonstrate the absolute turmoil I was in and the effect it was having on me mentally by being two people; it was more like a tug-of-war.

Luckily yet gradually over the years the extremes became less extreme, and the partying finally came to a close. I wrote my first book, *If You Could Have Anything... What Would It Be?* just as I was taking my last drink and it chronicles my journey through addiction, the 10 -year abusive relationship I was in at the time, my bankruptcy as well as the six years I lived, worked and partied in Thailand.

I found a route out of all those difficulties, which is what I am sharing with you today, and it has taken me the past 20 years to formulate the process into a technique that I can finally articulate to a wide audience. This comes from three decades of experience; nearly 20 years of teaching yoga and meditation; over 10 years a Tibetan Buddhist and countless hours, days, weeks, months and years perfecting the approach through delivering the online programme, teaching classes, workshops and retreats on the subject.

What I realise is that I had to experience it all so that I can help others: **YOU**. Because how else can someone successfully guide another out of despair if they haven't first already experienced it? I wouldn't employ a business mentor who wasn't already successful themselves, or take driving lessons from someone who cannot drive.

At the time I didn't know this, though, and the struggle sometimes seemed endless. Why did I drink until I blacked out? Or smoke until I was sick? Why did I stay with a man who called me a vile four-letter word everyday? There were times when I cried and asked, '*Why me?*'

Some days I would wake up with big puffy eyes and couldn't remember why I'd been crying all night. I risked everything one Christmas in Thailand when I bought 30 ecstasy tablets, hid them in my shoe, and drove 10 miles back to my house. If I had been caught I'd still be in a Thai jail today. More times than I can remember I woke up with 'the horrors', not remembering anything about the night before, getting phone calls from friends and acquaintances informing me exactly what trouble I had got myself into, and cringing with remorse and regret every time the phone rang. I would hide away in my house, frightened, timid and too ashamed to come out until it was dark.

Now I can see that I needed to learn those harsh lessons. I needed to suffer and struggle. All of it made me strong, made me fight, and out the other side I 'found myself'. I found the real me underneath the layer of drug-highs and do you know what, I liked what I found. And that was the beginning of the rest of my life, and what followed was a journey of self-discovery.
And it is this very path that I share with you now, exactly WHAT I did and HOW I changed my mind-set to one of unlimited abundance.

Have you ever learnt a new bit of information and therefore *'know'* it? Then over the course of the coming months and years you realise that the knowledge is not now merely on the surface of your mind, but has matured and deepened as you have *'become'* it.

This is my experience with the Law Of Attraction work. It came into my life over 10 years ago and I welcomed it with open arms. I absolutely got it. Or so I thought! Because it takes time for the *belief* to fully filter through our attitudes, beliefs, judgements, prejudices and conditioning. Back then I did know it on one level. However, now that information is very different because I've been *living* with it for such a long time. Then I became interested in quantum physics, which took me way beyond the Law Of Attraction to the next level of understanding ultimate reality; it was the natural next step for me, and the fact that science could prove what I was already experiencing made me very excited.

And we all have this process working throughout our lives. As we grow we learn to do so many things – walking, talking, eating, kissing, working, driving – that seem weird for the first time only for them to become second nature.

We drive on the other side of the road when we visit different countries and soon get used to everything being opposite. So this notion of new information seeping into our psyche and becoming absolutely second nature is not a new one.

I know struggle. I know hardship. I know despair. And I want you to know that wherever you are now, it's ok. There is hope for a bright, positive and happy future.

But it had to be that way; to have a reference point; to know how bad it can get so that you fully appreciate your new superpower once you harness it. And whatever you have done, wherever you find yourself now, you can draw a line under the sand and make the decision that enough is enough.
*This is why it's so important to fill out the **_Beginning Questionnaire_** in the Introduction Chapter (see p. 14). If you haven't done this already, please do so now so that you can get the very most out of this journey.*

The Spectrum of Addiction
Just like autism I believe that addiction has a spectrum. We are all on it somewhere ranging from very mild habits to full blown addictions. And once we learn in some detail how our brains are made up, we can pull ourselves

out of the trap of a destructive addiction and bring it more into balance within the scale.

My job in this book is to give you this information in an easy to understand form; the very knowledge that has set me, and many in the Quantum Sobriety community, free.

I sat at the more extreme end of the addiction range with what society terms an 'addictive personality'.

For us it is pretty black and white: drink until you black out or don't drink at all, there is no grey area in between. However for others it is not like this, the middle way is sufficient and an ability to 'switch off' after a drink or two is possible.

But we are not just talking about substance abuse here. Once we harness our Quantum Superpower we can turn around the imbalance that is created from anger, fear and other destructive emotions and fed into all areas of our lives.

When you think about it when does a healthy habit turn into a destructive addiction? An Olympic athlete needs to be addicted to their sport to be at the top of their game, ceasing all other commitments to allow them time to train hard for competitions. Equally an entrepreneur works long hours and is always thinking about their business to be at the pinnacle of their industry. Are they healthy? Society deems they are and we admire their drive, persistence and success. BUT it does become destructive when the athlete injures themselves or the business owner doesn't see their children. Then harm is being done and the balance has been compromised.

What Is This Superpower?

I knew I was onto something special when my life changed from one of despair, struggle and scarcity to being full of happiness, money, success and *ease*.

The shift was so huge that everyone in my life noticed it, not just me, and I found more and more people were asking me what my secret was and if I could 'bottle it'. I started to collect the pieces to this puzzle 20 years ago, but it has taken me this long to put them all together with the final fragment only falling into place relatively recently.

And with this last wedge of insight in place the superpower revealed itself in its entirety and finally I can share it with the world.

It has eight parts, which we will explore in detail in Part Two of this book: **'The Quantum Qualities'**

On their own they are amazing enough, but put these eight qualities *together* and you have a superpower; an unstoppable force that will take you wherever you want to go in life.

It started off nearly 20 years ago for me when I took an extended holiday, lived on a beach for a few months, took off my watch and realised I could tell the time during daylight hours by the shadow of the sun, and at night by the location of the Orion constellation in the sky.

Up until that time I had worn a watch every day of my adult life and so the revelation that I could do this task via nature blew me away and was what initially opened my eyes to there being more to my life than my then reality.

From that point in the mid-1990s I was changed. I had placed one foot on the path and begun my journey, this journey that has changed my trajectory forever. And you are also already on this route just by having this book in your hands. It is no coincidence. And it doesn't matter where you are on your life expedition, at the beginning or half way along, you've started and I promise it's going to get really exciting now that you've said YES to an enhanced way of living.

I am going to share my secrets. How I unlocked my potential and accessed my superpower, a superpower that we all have. Yours is waiting for you to claim. *Want to get started?*

The Science Of Meditation

'Wisdom is born from meditation.
Not to meditate is loss.
Know the difference between gain and loss.
Make the choice to walk where wisdom grows'
The Dhammapada

There is a common cord that runs throughout this system and is what binds the whole concept together and makes it a superpower: **Meditation**.

I first attempted it 20 years ago, and was absolutely rubbish!

'My mind is too busy.'
'This is so boring.'
'I don't think I will ever be able to do it.'

These were just some of my beliefs at the time, and to be honest I came up with excuse after excuse not to meditate in the beginning.

It has only been during the last 10 years that I really 'got' it, and meditation is now central to me being happy, healthy, successful and sober. To be perfectly honest I actually feel like a different person from who I was 20, 10 or even two years ago, and when I look back it pains me to see how unhappy I was. But how can my life be so incomparable to 20 years ago?

Well the answer is that I have *changed* my brain. I quite literally AM NOT the same person.

Testing has been carried out over the last 15 years with MRI scans, showing pictures and videos of the brain whilst highly accomplished practitioners are meditating inside the machine. These images have sent back information on exactly how the brain reacts during meditation by tracing paths of activity in the different areas of this complex organ.

Then results from an EEG (electroencephalogram) add brain wave patterns to the mix giving a clear, precise reading of exactly what is going on. *In the true flavour of this book being non-academic, I am not going to complicate things with too much scientific detail. However, at the back of this book there is reference to various relevant studies should you wish to delve a little deeper.*

Left Prefrontal Cortex – The Happiness Hotspot
The indisputable results time and time again are that the brain changes, activity is moving around, with the left prefrontal cortex becoming stimulated during meditation. This is the area of the brain where if high levels of activity are found, people report feeling happy, content, alert, enthusiastic and having a lot of energy.

The exact reverse is true for the right prefrontal cortex: subjects with a high level of activity here report feelings of unease, stress, worry and sadness. If you are feeling depressed or suffering with depression then it is very likely that the right prefrontal cortex will show a high level of activity, with the left side quiet.

Each of us has a balance of left and right prefrontal cortex activity as our normal setting. When we feel happy this balance will shift to the left, and when sad to the right. Most of us are not even aware of this happening and how our moods are affecting our life, but now that you are I am going to give you methods to swing that pendulum to the left, and keep it there.

With training (meditation) this is exactly what we are doing, and science backs it up. You can reset your 'normal' setting to further up the scale towards the left permanently, and this is what I have done and why I don't feel like the person I used to be (because I'm actually not).

Rather than crying everyday and feeling depressed, I am grateful for everything in my life; my default setting forever improved; *and I can assure you I am never going back.*

So What Is Going On In The Brain?
Only 5% of our minds are conscious and 95% are subconscious*. Our conscious mind is the home of logic and reason, and analyses everything. For most of us that means we are living the majority of our lives from the smallest fraction of our brains. So what does the other

95% of our mind do? Well this is where our beliefs live, and they breed our behaviours, perceptions, habits and, ultimately, addictions.

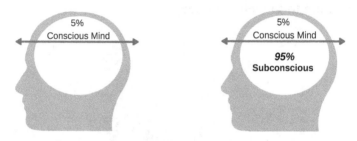

Dr Joe Dispenza, Breaking The Habit Of Being Yourself

When we meditate, we are accessing our subconscious mind. On the surface 5% we can only analyse whereas deep below the 5% line we touch in on our innate consciousness. There is quite a thick, tough line, however, between the two, and I hear so many people complain that it just 'isn't possible' for them to meditate, just as I felt at the beginning. But there is nothing wrong with their brains. They have simply given up at the first sign of resistance. Yes the line between the conscious and subconscious minds is difficult to penetrate for some, but the reward if you stick with it is freedom and enlightenment; can you afford *not* to attempt it?

In our first two meditations of the programme we will walk down into our subconscious minds and make the connection with our conscious self. Our two worlds are then forever linked as we become 'Super-Conscious'.

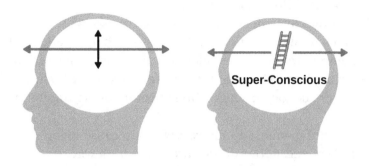

Super-Conscious

When we live our lives from the top 5% of our minds we react instantly without a thought. It's like the outside is bombarding us with questions, demands, stresses, anxieties, responsibilities, expectations and difficulties and it all starts to really weigh us down. We do our utmost best to stay on top of everything but it is easy to get overwhelmed, and we end up feeling like we've had arrows directed at us all day and we look somewhat like a pincushion.

Most of my life I've been living this way and it's exhausting. This method is all about ease and effortlessness, and trust me *everything* is about to get easier for you.

The Mind / Body Connection

Our bodies are not separate from our minds, which is so obvious to me now, but society seems to have overlooked this important point. Just like my car doesn't drive off on its own when I sit behind the wheel, so too our bodies need instructions from our brains before doing *anything*.

We do not manifest an illness without a cause being FIRST created in our minds. It is the body's way of communicating with us,

'Hey, things are out of balance and I'm trying to get a message to you!'
'Oi, you're stressed, slow down. If you don't I'm going to play up and give you a nasty disease/broken leg/fever to get you to spend the day/week/month in bed!'

Why do we not listen when this happens and take stock of what is out of balance and address it? Whatever is going on in our minds is being translated immediately and directly to our bodies through chemicals and hormones.

First Taste of Science

I wasn't taught any of this at school, and have spent most of my life completely in the dark about *how* my body works. My outer environment has always been where I've placed my attention, and I've reacted to external people, places and environments until just a few years ago.

In meditation we take the outside layer of life off, and sit for a period of time with ourselves, who we *really* are. Not who we pretend to be, or would like to be, but us at the most basic level. I have always called this part of us our 'essence' but you can call it soul, spirit, God, Christ, Allah, Buddha Nature, consciousness, the 'I-Am' source or any other name that resonates. For the purpose of ease I will refer to this state throughout the book as essence.

The more we connect to who we really are at this level the more we really know ourselves, what makes us tick, what makes us happy. We can even notice when we are out of balance *before* we get sick. However, our demanding lives often prevent us from sitting on our meditation cushion and if I had a pound for every time someone said to me that their minds were too active for meditation or they were too busy to meditate, I'd be an obscenely rich lady. What that person is really saying to me is,

'Meditation is not a priority to me'
'I don't realise how much I'm holding myself back by not making the commitment to meditate everyday, no matter if it is a 'good' or 'bad' session that day'
'I am saying no to life'
'I don't understand the importance of a daily practice'

And it is this lack of understanding and education around meditation that I'd like to clarify and fill in some gaps.

For the person who says their minds are too busy: ALL of our minds start out that way. No one starts meditation in the beginning and can still their minds for hours at a time; it takes practice and perseverance. And just like a musician clocks up hours of rehearsal before a performance, a meditator cannot expect instant results. Think of any athlete – do you think they are at the top of their field without practice? This is often where most fall at the first hurdle (excuse the pun), giving up before they've really started, however, with the relevant information contained in this book you will have a really good chance; there are some very powerful meditations contained in the following chapters.

And for the individual who says they do not have enough time, we are going to start with just five minutes of practice each day. Who cannot find that? There are 288 opportunities every day to meditate for five minutes! I have spent the last 20 years meditating, 10 of those extensively and, therefore, have the results of that. And it is irrefutably *guaranteed* that you can transform your life too if you just jiggle things around a bit and make time for meditation everyday. Your brain *has* to change.

Do you want to be happy?
Do you want more energy?
Do you want to have a clear unfoggy head?
Do you want to have a body that is healthy?
Do you want more abundance in all areas of your life?
Do you want to feel content and at peace with yourself?

All of this is possible. It is a tried and tested system: You put the time and effort in and you will see results. If you don't, you won't.

Think of someone who is overweight, doesn't exercise and eats loads of junk food. That person starts to eat more healthily and exercise, and the weight falls off. It's obvious; there is a cause and an effect. But the weight doesn't disappear overnight; there is an on-going intention, commitment and goal.

Exactly the same is happening with meditation and if you don't start today then you continue to hold yourself back from the amazing life that is waiting for you.

Anyway lecture over (for now!) and back to the science. Once I had noticed fundamental shifts in my beliefs, perceptions and outer circumstances I began to delve a little deeper into what was changing in my brain.

Hello Neurons

I then did the unthinkable; I started to research neuroscience and my family thought this non-academic had gone bonkers. But it fascinated me and I began to understand precisely what was happening to my brain when I meditated, felt stressed or got an addictive urge.

I was intrigued to learn about neural networks and how every thought that we have sends a message via nerve cells, called neurons, along a chain. They 'fire' an electrical impulse to their next-door neighbour and a connection is made (synapse). However they can also fire to multiple locations so one solitary thought can be magnified, like the ripple effect of a pebble thrown into a lake.

And if we have the same thought over and over again these connections form a long-term relationship, and voila! We have created a habit or memory.

> *'When neurons fire together, they wire together'*
> Donald Hebb

It is a little like digging a trench; every time you repeat a thought you are digging a little deeper,

'I'm ugly.'
'I'm not a morning person.'
'I've never got enough money.'
'Why does it always happen to me?'
'I don't deserve to be happy.'
'I want another drink.'
'I hate my job.'
'I'm bored.'

These thoughts are quite literally *becoming* us, and then we wonder why it is difficult to change the pattern and a lot of us believe that this is who we have become and that we cannot ever change. *This is absolutely not true.* We can change our brain.

But we have to be very careful because we react on the most hardwired neural networks in the brain, which means we do the same things over and over again. Can you look back and notice that you have had the same kind of relationship time and time again? Or find yourself in the same situation of self-flagellation, abuse or an addictive cycle? Maybe you order the very same dish every time you go to your favourite restaurant?

The brain also builds up an associated memory within the networks it has made so that thoughts, feelings, places or even smells have a relationship with one another. For instance I only have to listen to a certain song to think of a particular person, or visit a place to remember a specific night out and the conversation that was had even though it was years ago. For someone who has been cheated on they may now associate love with disappointment and/or anger so that when they even think about love they experience anger, pain or sorrow. An addicted person will associate the time of day, a meal, a person, or occasion with their substance of choice leaving them seemingly no option but to partake in their poison.

I met someone who had a severe allergy to cats. It turns out that towards the end of their relationship she perceived her ex-husband chose the family cat over her, and hey presto she has a negative reaction whenever there is a cat around. Cat lady wasn't conscious of the connection but once we had that conversation and brought it up out of her subconscious mind she completely got it and began working on resolving the negative association. What connections are you making? What have you hardwired? Are you even aware of doing this?

I know I wasn't up until a few years ago, and immediately I could see how one negative thought could poison the brain and how a lifetime of addiction to drugs and alcohol had damaged my brain. When I recall the first days of giving up any of my addictions, the pull back to doing the very thing that I didn't want to do was so horribly strong. Now I understood that I had literally programmed myself to react in that way. The really awesome news is that we can reverse this. Just as we create negative associations, we can also establish positive ones.

The Rush Of Chemicals
However, before we get to the technique there is another layer to the science of the mind: for every thought that we have, there is an outcome chemically in our body. We cannot stop this from happening but we can change our thoughts and, therefore, the result. (More about *how to* in later chapters). First, let's understand what is going on....

We have different chemicals for every emotion that we experience: chemicals for anger; love; lust; sadness; happiness; victimisation, etc... When we trigger an emotion in our brain, a signal is sent to the hypothalamus gland which is like a kitchen creating, brewing and concocting a myriad of recipes for every occasion. Once a 'match' has been found the chemical is released into the bloodstream and around the body to find a corresponding cell where it will be able to perform its designated task.

Every cell has thousands of receptors, which are sensors (or like a keyhole) waiting for the right chemicals (key) to arrive. And there is only one key per lock. Once the specific chemical has found a matching receptor they lock together with a signal being sent into the cell, which then reorganises and is responsible for how we are feeling and behaving right now and always.

For example, a ferry full of people is on its way to an island. The island has a pier where the boat will dock and visitors alight. Our cells have the receptor sites built on the outside ready for chemicals to also be received.

Five people get off the boat. They all have a completely different agenda for being on the island:

1. The first is a member of staff who quickly makes his way to a door marked private.

2. The next person heaves a heavy suitcase up the hotel lawn and into the reception area ready to check-in.

3. One person gets off who is a day tourist who walks up the beach and along the path towards the lighthouse.

4. The final passenger gets off to stretch their legs but then boards the boat again to go on to the next stop.

5. The captain briefly disembarks to help everyone off.

Each receptor site has a specific requirement that it is searching for. As chemicals move through the bloodstream the receptor is watching and waiting for the right one to come along. From the above example there is also a response for each person on the boat:

1. The kitchen staff are pleased that their colleague has arrived with an ingredient that is needed for dinner.

2. Someone from reception is expecting the guest's arrival.

3. The day tourist buys souvenirs from the shop.

4. This passenger's loved one is waiting at the next stop.

5. More customers are waiting for the captain to take them back to the mainland.

And once the receptor cells find a match they pull the chemical towards them, to dock and receive its information.

EXAMPLES of the mind–body chemical reaction:

1. You are walking through security at the airport and even though you have nothing illegal on your person you can feel your heart start to quicken, your palms become sweaty, and your eyes dart nervously from side to side. Your brain has perceived a threat and begun a chemical reaction throughout your body; your brain has also made the association of jail with memories of TV shows that you've seen when someone gets caught.

2. You are sexually aroused and as thoughts of your suitor cascade through your mind a whole host of reactions have been put into play with hormones being released. Areas of your body that are far away from your brain begin to change and get ready for what is about to happen.

3. You realise that you left the cooker on and you are now on the train to work. It feels like you have been slapped and that all the blood in your body has drained into the floor. Your heartbeat accelerates as an image of the fire brigade at your house flashes into your mind.

What this means is that because of the chemical release we now FEEL the way we are THINKING: the mind and body are one. The body does not do any of this on its own without first being directed by the master that is the mind.

Let's go back to the conversations I listed a bit earlier:

'I'm ugly.'
'I'm not a morning person.'
'I've never got enough money.'
'Why does it always happen to me?'

'I don't deserve to be happy.'
'I want another drink.'
'I hate my job.'
'I'm bored.'

Once we add the chemical reaction that the brain has signalled to the body, these beliefs become even more hardwired than before to the extent that they become our personality; we accept these statements as truth because it's all we've ever known. And the mind can only see what we believe is possible. Ouch. So we are going round and round in circles, not knowing how on earth to change our reality; knowing that there is something more, something else but having no insight into what that is or how to achieve it.

Take someone who has always suffered with low self-esteem. Every time they have a thought about not being worthy of the job, relationship, happiness or love they release certain chemicals into their body. This becomes so normal to them over their lifetime that this chemical dance desensitises the cells and the feeling of unworthiness actually becomes *pleasurable*, and this person will now seek out or create situations to meet their chemical needs.

Trying to change a lifetime of negative self-belief whether it's low self-esteem, guilt, anger or fear is for the body exactly the same as going through withdrawal from drugs or alcohol. This is why the Quantum Sobriety approach works no matter what you are addicted to, because the brain works in exactly the same way for each.

So you see the mind really is where it's at, which is why meditation is the key to making any changes you want to experience in your life. What is the point of continuingly cutting a weed down without pulling it out by its root? Perhaps this is what you have been doing over the last few years. I know it took me a long time to finally realise that I had to go back to the beginning, where the problem arose, and tackle my imbalances from their source.

Now that we have a basic understanding of what is going on in our brains, let's take a break from science and delve into the world of Buddhism which contains meditation as its foundation....

The Result Is The Path

'You are what your deep, driving desire is
As your desire is, so is your will
As your will is, so is your deed
As your deed is, so is your destiny'
Brihadaranyaka Upanishad

Many of the western studies of accomplished meditators have been conducted on Tibetan Buddhist monks, for they have had a lifetime of daily intensive practice within their monastic life. They are capable of unbelievable mind control and so make excellent subjects.

I was introduced to Tibetan Buddhism in 2005 whilst I was studying yoga in India. I'd been living full-time in Thailand for five years already which is a Buddhist country, but had never been drawn to 'being' a Buddhist whilst there. There are of course many different forms of Buddhism, with Thailand part of the Theravada school and Tibet belonging to the Vajrayana lineage; each one approaches the same subject from a slightly different angle, and I guess that was why in Thailand it didn't appeal.

Whilst in India, a friend took me to see His Holiness Karmapa, who I'd never heard of at the time so had no insight or expectation of what was about to happen. That day is one I will never forget. It was the first time I had been in the presence of an enlightened being; someone so highly evolved that it is like they are looking straight into your soul, and watching every thought as it crosses your mind. The whole experience took my breath away and I hardly said a word for the rest of the day after meeting HH Karmapa. After that I went back to his then twice weekly public audiences for my remaining time in India, which was about five months. Sometimes he gave a teaching, where I hung on to every single word translated by an interpreter and furiously wrote down everything he said , and the rest of the time he simply gave a blessing.

The connection to HH Karmapa is something I find hard to explain because it is so deep and unshaking, yet unfathomable to put into a sentence. It's at a soul level, and I knew it the instant I saw him as I've *never* experienced anything like that before. One year later I returned to India and took refuge with HH Karmapa who gave me the Buddhist name, 'Karma Choekyi' meaning 'of the Dharma', which translates as 'of the teachings'. He must have known I was a communicator of information!

The Buddha knew that anything was possible, for he sat under the Bodhi tree and vowed not to move from there until he gained enlightenment; nobody had done this before, but he knew that he could do it. The Buddha teaches not to believe anything unless you can prove it, to not have blind faith in someone but to find out for yourself. So he would teach what he knew to be true, but it is up to each of us to discover if it is also our own truth.

As Buddhists we develop 'Bodhichitta', an awakened heart (with a balance of wisdom and compassion), and a wish to end the suffering of all beings. A Bodhisattva is a person who has made a commitment to assist others in finding peace within themselves and freedom from suffering. A Bodhisattva does not have to be a Buddhist, just have a heart wide open with compassion flowing out. Well-known individuals like Gandhi, Mother Theresa and HH Dalai Lama are obvious but there are many Bodhisattvas in our society right now, most of whom work tirelessly under the radar doing remarkable work.

Finding Your Own Religion
Please don't worry, you don't have to become a Buddhist to gain your Quantum Superpower! Although this particular practice has fed my own spiritual growth, we each find faith somewhere different and must honour our own path and religion. Faith in something, whether it is God, Allah, Spirit, Buddha Nature, pure consciousness, the 'I-AM', Source, Fate or the Universe forms the foundation of our personal happiness and abundance. All faiths have meditation or prayer as the backbone of their system, so please replace the word Buddha/Buddhism with one that sits more comfortably with you if you prefer. Within the Quantum Sobriety community we have members from all faiths and none; everyone is welcome and no one excluded.

Evolving
Being in a room with highly evolved souls who are putting in hours of meditation daily inspires us to believe that more is possible, and motivates us to prioritise our own meditation practice. Take a look around and you will see people further down the path than you are; people whom you admire, and would like to be like. Go to teachings, talks and lectures with them. They have so much Bodhichitta overflowing from them that they are able to offer it out to us just by being in their presence, and we should never give up an opportunity to soak it up; learn from them and therefore understand ourselves and what's possible, better.

'We should be aware that there are beings who are more advanced than we are, who have more realisation than we do. Their very existence shows us that a more enlightened state of mind is possible, that there is a possibility to receive their inspiration, to open up to their influence.'
Ringu Tulku Rinpoche

Deity Meditation

My Buddhist practice over the last 10 years has been Chenrezig, who is the deity of compassion. During the meditation you imagine yourself as Chenrezig, and start to generate compassion within yourself and give it out to everyone. In this way we become the embodiment of the deity and it becomes easier to create compassion not just during your meditation but all through the day as well. My experience is that just as with meditation, feeling compassion is also like a muscle that you must exercise to strengthen or it will atrophy. Growing up I was incredibly selfish and as a young adult overly confident, so for me compassion has always been a trait that I struggled to create. But I was naturally drawn to the practice, instinctively knowing that what I found so difficult was for sure going to be a powerful teacher, and it has softened me beyond belief. It is beautiful, and I look forward to my yearly pilgrimage to Samye Ling Monastery in Scotland for the annual Nyungney retreat where we practise the 1,000-armed version of Chenrezig.

Thousand-armed Chenrezig is a purification practice hence the alternate days of silence and fasting (even brushing your teeth is not permitted on the fasting days) with prayers, mantras, meditations and prostrations in each of the three daily sessions. The effects are profound and last the whole year for me, and over the years of doing this sacred practice the teaching contained within this book and programme has become clearer and clearer to me.

At the end of each session we say the following prayer, which I say out loud every morning to set my intention for the coming day,

'Jang choob sem ni rim po cheh
Ma Kyeh pa nam kyeh gyoor chig
Kyeh pa nyam pa meh pa tang
Gong neh gong too p'el war dzo'

Translated into English:

'The Precious Bodhicitta Thought
In whom it has not been born
May it arise
In whom it has arisen may it not diminish
But grow and flourish'

The Lotus

Every single Buddha statue, painting or image that you see depicts Buddha sitting upon a lotus flower. This represents the fact that we all have 'Buddha Nature' within us. A lotus grows through mud to reach the surface of the water to flower, and it is mud that gives it the sustenance so that it can become strong. So it doesn't matter where you are in the moment of reading this book, or what you have done in the past. Every moment is an opportunity to touch in on your Buddha Nature (or whatever you want to call it) and make the connection to self. Just because you have done something bad in the past does not mean that you cannot be a good person in the future.

I have talked already about what I have called 'essence' in the previous chapter, with Buddha Nature being one and the same thing. In fact in every religion or belief system there is a feeling or ambiance of a 'higher power', which is what everyone aims to connect to. Some religions see it outside of themselves whilst others within, but it seems to be a common concept.

*'This is the Vajrayana way of practising: **'using the result as the path.'** Of course, we can't totally understand or imagine what being Chenrezig feels like or what an enlightened being is thinking about, but through our studies and through our limited knowledge, we can imagine what it might be like. We just become Chenrezig, almost as if we let our mind dissolve or mix with Chenrezig. We don't analyse this process; there's no place for thoughts, concepts and doubts. We just dissolve into Chenrezig, become Chenrezig, feel that Chenrezig and we have become one, and rest in that state. We let our mind 'be' Chenrezig and remain in this uncontrived nature of our mind.'*

Ringu Tulku Rinpoche

When I first read the words in his book, '**using the result as the path**', I quite literally felt that I had been spiritually slapped; this was exactly what I was already teaching in my manifestation sessions with vision boards (more on that later).

One Thousand Arms: All Giving

The image that we see of Chenrezig is steeped in symbolism with him standing, of course, on a lotus flower. He stands with one foot in each world: the human realm, and that of the gods. He has **eight** main arms each depicting a different meaning: wishing; cleansing; teaching; protecting, for example, with the remaining 992 arms all in the gesture of giving. Each year as I took part in the Nyungney retreat another part of the puzzle unfurled, but I still couldn't quite work out how to put all of the pieces together. However, finally at the retreat in 2015 it did all become clear, the very last fragment revealing itself and I knew exactly how I was going to arrange it all.

As I looked at the main influences in my life a very distinct pattern emerged. The number EIGHT. And even before I had realised this I had already mapped out EIGHT insights that seemed to form the template for what I taught. This is what the Buddhist masters charted:

The Eight-Fold Path
One of Buddha's principal teachings:

1. **Right View:** seeing reality as it is, not just as it appears to be
2. **Right Intention:** of renunciation, freedom and harmlessness
3. **Right Speech:** speaking the truth in a non-hurtful way
4. **Right Action:** not to kill, injure, lie or cheat
5. **Right Livelihood:** helping others in your work
6. **Right Effort:** making an effort to improve
7. **Right Mindfulness:** clear consciousness. Aware of the present reality within oneself
8. **Right Concentration:** meditation

The Eight Limbs Of Yoga
Most people in the west only know of the third 'limb' of yoga – Asana, discipline of the body – but this forms only one of eight parts to the whole that is yoga. The word 'yoga' means yoke or union.

1. **Yama:** how we relate to the world
2. **Niyama:** how we relate to ourselves
3. **Asana:** discipline of the body
4. **Pranayama:** control of energies
5. **Pratyahara:** withdrawal of senses from external objects
6. **Dharana:** concentration / visualisation
7. **Dhyana:** undisturbed flow of thought
8. **Samadhi:** oneness, no separation

Building A Bridge

These two philosophies have been part of my life for a very long time and in history for the past few millennia. They are still amazingly current but don't speak our present day language.

A bridge between two worlds became more and more clear, and it all really started to come together when I realised that every part of my world was saying the same thing:

YOU CREATE YOUR OWN DESTINY

- Firstly I had been creating vision boards
- Secondly I was practising Vajrayana Buddhism
- Thirdly I had discovered how the brain works
- And finally I got to know the wonderful and weird world of quantum physics

And all four of these paths were leading to the same garden; one of fertile ground where I could plant whatever seeds I chose, which grew to be my wildest hopes and dreams manifested. All of a sudden my whole life was compatible, which was a huge relief because I had spent quite a few years feeling torn between my faith and what I was doing for work; which had seemed to be so materialistic (the manifestation business), when most Buddhists that I met seemed to be neck deep in suffering and renunciation! At last my whole life was congruent.

Buddhist Wedding

Dom and I got married at the monastery in Scotland in 2011 with Akong Rinpoche giving the full Buddhist blessing. He came over from Tibet in the 1960s and set up Samye Ling, which was the very first Tibetan monastery to open outside of Asia. He also 'found' HH Karmapa when he was a small boy in Tibet so the connections between them and me are numerous.

The wedding service came as quite a surprise to Dom and I, with us exchanging wide-eyed glances at each other when Rinpoche bestowed upon us all the happiness, wealth and material possessions that we could ever want or need. He kept saying the word 'everything' (Rinpoche was actually speaking in Tibetan, and had someone translating into English), and in that moment I realised that there was nothing wrong with having possessions, as long as the *intention* to have them came from the right place. Inner peace and happiness of course is more important, *but there is nothing wrong with having things.* It was literally a mind-blowing moment.

The Science Of Buddhism

Buddhism has always had a deep interest in science with the Abhidharma (Buddhist philosophical text) being written two thousand years ago. Its psychology professes a scale of emotions, with a student progressed in spiritual practice not feeling the hold of destructive emotions or becoming overwhelmed by the changes in their life. The more meditation the student practises the more *Sukha* they experience, a Sanskrit term for happiness and contentment that comes from the inside out and is not dependent on outer circumstances. This would also tie in exactly with the practitioner's set point of their left/right prefrontal cortex pendulum. So it would appear that science and Buddhism are very much on the same page.

Relative and Ultimate Reality

In Buddhism there are two realities: the reality that is what is really going on in the world, and the reality that is what we are attached to. Ultimate and relative realities respectively. As we saw earlier the very first teaching in the Buddha's Eight Fold Path is 'Right view: seeing reality as it is, not just as it appears to be'. When we are triggered to drink we have an internal battle going on:

Relative reality = I want a drink now because it's the easiest thing to do
Ultimate reality = I do not actually want that drink because it is harming me

So when we can see clearly we realise that the last drink is causing the need for the next, but when we are caught up in the moment and the desire, it is difficult to see the bigger picture. Tibetan Buddhism is about the search for ultimate truth; to realise that nothing is fixed and everything is to play for, which is also exactly where quantum physics takes us compared to the sciences of old.

'Physics deals with relative reality
Quantum physics speaks of ultimate reality
Therefore, spirituality can at last be explained by science.'
Tibetan Buddhist Monk

Science And Buddhism Meet
His Holiness the Dalai Lama is greatly interested in science and has been involved in the Mind and Life Institute's on-going meetings since 1987. Buddhist and Western scientific perspectives are discussed over differing subjects such as 'The Science of Altruism', 'Does our Perception Mirror Reality?', 'How the Languages We Speak Shape the Ways We Think' and 'Mental Training: Impact on Neuronal, Cognitive, and Emotional Plasticity', with the outcome being new programmes devised to aid more people in their search for happiness. It seems that I'm not the only one who has seen the similarities between the two perspectives. See the reference

section for more information and links to the above conversations.

Could It Be?

What I am starting to fathom is that Jesus, Buddha and the Mayans, etc... may have discovered the world of quantum physics. Obviously they would not have called it that but it makes a lot of sense to me that they could 'see' things that others couldn't, and used their minds in expanded ways that were ahead of their times.

In Tibetan Buddhism the high Lamas or Rinpoches (teachers) leave messages about their next incarnation; predicting their own birthplace, parents' names and such like. Their minds are highly evolved enough through meditation to make this possible, and it shows us just how powerful the mind is when trained.

The current Dalai Lama is the 14th incarnation of himself, but it is the Karmapa being in his 17th body who holds the longest lineage. The very first Karmapa was born in 1110 and since then the teachings and the practices have remained the same; all Tibetan Buddhism has a very direct and pure lineage. This means my own practice is the same as it was over a thousand years ago, and I feel very privileged to be part of its history.

There are many stories of the realised Lamas being able to be in two places at the same time, and predicting future events. And once we begin to comprehend quantum physics, that may not seem like such an impossibility.

Enter The Quantum

Quantum theory was the very last part of the puzzle for me but actually has been the catalyst for the coalescence of all of the knowledge I've been given. And I feel it is really important to show that this superpower is steeped in science rather than a fluffy world of 'woo woo'! In the quantum field anything is possible, something that I have always known (hence the title of my first book) but couldn't prove, until my journey down the quantum rabbit hole gave me all the answers I've ever been searching for.

What is exciting is that this area of science is so new with more and more findings, understandings and studies being discovered all the time. Just 20 years ago it was believed that the neurons in our brains from birth were all we would have during the course of our life, meaning any degeneration through illness or substance abuse was irreversible; that we were 'set' for life.

Neuroplasticity

Brain science has come a long way over the last two decades and now we know that the brain is constantly changing due to our experiences, altering both through new connections with existing neurons, as we saw in the meditation chapter, plus creating brand new neurons. I think living in this era of discovery is unbelievably exciting and the fact that in my lifetime we have learned so much about being human; like proving that we live in a *limitless* world.

Each connection between two cells creates a memory, so when you start to change the pathways and make new ones you are rewiring your brain and becoming a different version of yourself. No wonder I feel like a different person when I look back 20 years to the addicted, unhealthy, struggling Jo, because I have changed tremendously. However, the memory of who I was will always be available and that information gets stored away, *and we call this wisdom*.

Becoming The Observer

This concept completely blew my mind when it finally clicked into place. I didn't connect with the sciences at school but then again they were not teaching this, because they didn't know it yet. Maybe I would have become an academic if I had been taught the unbelievable fact that an atom is made up of 0.00001% matter and 99.99999% energy. Bear in mind that you are made up entirely of atoms, so this means that you are 99% energy! And energy is not fixed; *it is constantly changing*. Once we can get our heads around this we realise that to fight *against* change (do you?) is like going to war with ourselves, which is exactly what a harmful addiction is achieving.

So can you see that by remaining *in* your addiction you are going against your nature? You need to stop looking back to where you have always been, and with courage look forwards to where you want to go. Harness the quantum field all around you; it is gently nudging you 'outwards'. The universe is ever expanding, meaning this expansion is inherent in us; we are unlimited and every single possibility is available to us; all we have to do is believe.

Matter is a circumstance of energy, meaning us energy beings control matter. Rather than feeling that your outer environment (matter) is controlling you, realise that YOU are in control of it. I know that up until now it's been the wrong way around – NOW is the time to flip it the right way and make life EASY for yourself by going *with* nature rather than against it.

Scientists have discovered that when no one is looking at it an electron disappears, in fact it is everywhere and nowhere all at the same time, and it is *only* when we observe it that it shows up. There has to be an observer for something to happen, therefore it is *consciousness* that is the observer. What is even more exciting is that before we observe anything there are an infinite number of possibilities, *everything is possible at this stage*, so we are *choosing* the option that we want. Once we have selected this reality by observing, it has to manifest (whether we like it or not). In science language, quantum physics calls this the 'collapse of the wave function' or the 'observer effect'. When a particle is not being observed it acts differently, as a *wave* of probability, and once we have observed it it will *collapse* into an actual experience. The particle CANNOT do this by itself, so we are affecting the outcome.

'Aha'

When I fully comprehended this information for the first time I held my head in my hands muttering 'oh my god, oh my god' for the next three days; it blew my mind! And from what I already knew about the make-up of the brain, I was quite literally witnessing the formation of new synapses in my grey matter; it's these 'Aha' moments that we have that form new neural networks, so we want more of them please!

It still blows my mind every time I think about it; that science can back up the vision board, visualisations, transcending addiction and the manifestation of the life you've always dreamed of. All the things I have believed for many years but didn't understand the science of *how* it was happening. And now I know the how; that everything that exists is made up of atoms, neurons and particles; *everything is connected*. Therefore everything has the potential to collapse into the reality that we choose and it is possible to alter our lives, *from this moment onwards*, in a positive way.

What Do You Believe?
So if every possibility is available to you what are you creating right now? What do you believe? Each potential in every situation is available to you and it is your consciousness that perceives what it believes is possible. What reality are you choosing today when you collapse the next wave of potential?

We can only experience what we believe is possible

As you read these words can you feel yourself expanding with the knowledge? Is your mind/body saying YES, let's get started? Or are you recoiling from the responsibility of it all and saying,

'That can't be true'

Only you have the power to collapse your own wave of possibilities; whatever you are believing in this moment you are creating, it has to be like that whether you like it or not.

Quantum Magic

The quantum field confirmed everything that I had already suspected in my search for freedom. But I hadn't any idea that magic was in fact real until I came across 'superposition'. Would you believe me when I said that a particle *can* be in numerous locations *at the same time?* As crazy as it sounds, it is true. When we are not observing it a particle can spread itself out in multiple positions, but as soon as we observe it, the particle will appear where we are looking. It took me eight years since I first heard that information to take it on fully. In the beginning my brain just *couldn't* quantify it, but finally I am willing to accept this magic as true because in that time I have witnessed how using this concept can change your life forever.

And of course superposition verifies what the Tibetan Buddhist Lamas are doing. It's so crazy that we can prove this, can you believe it yet? There *is* magic all around us, and all we have to do is *accept* it to tap into its power.

Invisibility Cloak

Let's look at this from another angle. We've all read about Harry Potter and his invisibility cloak; a layer of protection that he places around him. The quantum realm is just like this, it's all around us and we have access to it *all of the time.* It is an energetic field like gravity, that we can't see, but it is surely there. And it waits for your command, it is intelligent, but it will *only* listen to *your* directive. The quantum field is like your best friend, always there for you, and it will do *anything* for you whatever you ask of it. In fact it is waiting more like a servant than a friend, it's a friendly servant, and your wish is its command.

What began nearly 10 years ago, teaching and talking about the Law Of Attraction has moved direction with this new information and is much smarter and more factual, for we now have evidence from the laboratory.

Pure Potential
Every possibility *already* exists as pure potential. Everything that you can imagine is out there in the quantum waiting for you to observe it.

- Perhaps you yearn to be fit and healthy. That reality already exists as pure potential in the quantum realm
- Or maybe you dream of becoming a yoga teacher? That reality also already exists as pure potential in the quantum realm
- What about not drinking anymore and being *happy* about the decision? That reality already exists as pure potential in the quantum realm too

Magic, eh? And all we have to do is observe it by believing that it's possible, to make it happen.

A Quantum Experiment
The annual Chenrezig fasting retreat that I have been attending for the last 10 years is meant to be difficult. The hunger, thirst and pain that comes from meditating for eight hours a day teaches us to be more mindful generally, and to focus on our practice. Also it cuts straight through to our belief system, by turning inward and looking at what is really going on we realise our resilience and strength.

I would like to take you on a journey through the years I have been practising Nyungney. As a writer I like to document interesting experiences, so have chronicled each retreat. The following are actual excerpts from my personal journal (unfortunately I couldn't find my journal from 2008 and my first contact with Nyungney, which I have to say was a total disaster!). Notice how my beliefs have totally transformed from a place of *'I can't do this'*, to *'I am enjoying and welcoming the experience'*.

2011

'This is dreadful, I'm starving, no one should be putting themselves through this, I don't think I can survive the night without water. I want to S C R E A M.'

'In the 1ˢᵗ session my back hurt, my mind played tricks with me and I really doubted I could make it.'

'I hope this retreat will get my meditation practice back into regularity.'

2012

'Still in shock that I put my alarm on for 5 this morning and actually got up and had a shower – that's never happened before!'

'Have severe pain in my back and don't think I can continue with the practice, can't sleep, can't sit up straight in meditation, all I want to do is cry :'(helllllppppp'

'Last year I felt so fabulous after I got home and lost it all completely as soon as I had a drink…this year I will not let that happen.'

2013

'I have decided that I am going to 'come out' in a blog when I get back! This is actually such a big step for me as I've very much kept my Buddhism quiet, almost secret up until now. And it is so fitting as I finally in the last two days realise how important this is to me, how connected to the practice I am, and how I must honour this!!! And how strange that when I arrived on the first day of practice I seriously questioned if I belonged here, and if I was

going to start doing a different retreat instead every year, I asked Chenrezig the question and have most definitely been answered!'

2014

'I'm bored! I cannot believe I am here for 16 days, I don't think I can get through it, in fact, I might leave early. Yes I am definitely going to leave early'
(NB: I didn't leave early but I struggled throughout the whole 16 days)

2015

Wednesday: *'What a difference a year makes! I cannot believe how different I am. Normally I have scurried into bed after the last meditation session, at the very earliest opportunity, and slept for 12 hours (or tried to). Today I just don't need to do that, I feel really good, rather than weak, hungry and light headed.*
Rather than wish these fasting days away by going to bed as early as possible, this year I am going into this completely differently; I want to enjoy all of it; every pang of hunger; every session; every minute ☺ The struggle has gone!'
Friday: *'I am hungry but amazingly for the first time I am welcoming it. The uncomfortableness is what we are ultimately here for after all: so that we practise NO MATTER WHAT. Wow how profound!!'*
(Friday and Saturday were very difficult days)
Tuesday: *'I am totally amazed at the transformation that has happened to me. I am so much more willing to look discomfort in the eye rather than run as fast as I can in the opposite direction. Unbelievable! I love this practise!'*

2016

Saturday: *'Let's have some fun with the fasting days and create the most easeful and enjoyable experience yet. I am feeling strong and ready going into this retreat, and there is no weakness in me. Bring it on!'*

Wednesday: *'I've not eaten for 32 hours or had anything to drink in 23 hours; not even brushed my teeth. I've also not uttered a word for 23 hours. I am literally starving, but feel amazingly clear-headed and alive. I don't feel weak in any way because I have chosen to do this, to take on this suffering for others, to know real hunger, real thirst and real pain in my body. I know that at 7am tomorrow I will be given my first cup of hot water which will taste like heaven. My physical body will lift itself up towards the sky like a wilted plant after a watering, yet my mind is already that high from turning inward and realising itself. I love this practice, its differing layers, the inner joy I feel today, and the outer joy of food and water tomorrow that I will experience. I feel very lucky and very humble right now.'*

2017

'Day 6 of the Nyungney and day 5 of continuous silence; the first time I have chosen to do more silence than is required. And I actually love being quiet when everyone else is talking; it feels more difficult, more of a challenge, and I am totally ready for MORE.

And magic has happened today.

Something HUGE shifted and I know exactly what it is; I totally let go and settled into trust. I have felt around the edges of this the last couple of years, but this Nyungney has sealed it; I've finally jumped in. The resistance dropped instantly, all of the striving, wanting and needing, all gone.'

Can you see how my language has changed? How I expected to struggle so did in the early years? You can only experience what you believe to be true and that is so clear in my own journey.

Quantum Entanglement

It gets stranger still this quantum business. Now it's time to look at the bending of time and space, because the above quantum magic can be used anywhere meaning that we don't have to be right next to our desired outcome to affect it. For me the easiest way to comprehend this is to think about astronauts travelling outside of our gravitational pull. Time moves slower as gravity decreases, which means the astronauts on the International Space Station age slower than us with two feet on the ground. Once we have that in our minds we can go even further down the rabbit hole and look at what is possible for us mere Earthlings....

Quantum entanglement states that two particles that connect stay connected throughout time and space, meaning that if something happens to one then the other also feels it. Take identical twins; there are countless reports of one feeling the others' pain even when they are on opposite sides of the planet.

Distance Healing

This means that when doing Reiki healing (or similar) it is just as powerful whether patient and healer are in the same room, or far away from each other. Perhaps if they are not in the same room it could even be *more* powerful because the layer of potential resistance, or analytical mind isn't there; the intention gets to the patient unopposed.

Think 'Anything'

We are unlimited beings with unlimited potential outcomes and it's time for us to think bigger. We've all heard the term *'think outside the box'*, and now this saying is getting an upgrade: THINK ANYTHING because we have it ALL available to us, there are literally no limits (apart from the ones you might be having right now).

So let's look at how you have reacted to the above information. Do you think I'm mad? Are you saying the following to yourself?

'That doesn't apply to me.'
'I can't have anything.'

EXERCISE THREE: First Contact
Let's make contact with the quantum now.
Read this exercise through first and then put the book down.
Close your eyes and get comfortable.
Start to become aware of your breath coming into and out of your body.
Then notice how your body is feeling: your feet; legs; bottom sitting on the chair; back; arms; hands resting on your legs; neck and head. Is there any part of your body that is calling for your attention? Go to that part and see what is happening. Pain? Discomfort? Numbness? Pulsation?
Then start to think about all of the possibilities that are available to you in this very moment. Think as big as you dare.

OK, now write down exactly what you were thinking about, even if it seems irrelevant right now. Log your current thoughts, feelings, dreams and aspirations.
Where are you at in this moment? What do you believe is possible for the rest of your life? What message are you giving your quantum buddy?
Bring your hands to your chest in a prayer position.

Look down towards your heart and thank yourself for beginning this journey, and congratulations, you just got your first glimpse of your Quantum Superpower!

A World That Is Upside Down

So much in life is the opposite of what it should be; as we've seen in previous chapters we live our whole lives in just 5% of our minds, whereas we are about to find out just how amazing life can be when we access the relatively 'unknown' subconscious mind.

Many of us feel trapped in a 'set' life: chained to mediocrity; a job you hate; relationships that dull you; food that is killing you, with no way out. As you have already discovered, it is all about to change, and you must hold on tight. The journey is sometimes not an easy one so be warned that to get to the top and enjoy the stunning view, you are going to have to climb up a sometimes steep rock face but it is all going to be worth it. Get strapped in because now that you have the full background of where my knowledge and experience has come from, I would like to introduce to you the method for discovering your very own superpower.

It's time to find out about the first Quantum Quality.

Part Two
The Quantum Qualities

For each Quantum Quality I am going to ask you to make some notes so it may be a good idea to purchase a journal solely for this purpose. I started writing one many years ago and it is wonderful looking back years later to see how far you've come. You've already read some excerpts from mine in the last chapter from 2011, although I have writings from much further back; dark and drunken days that I am so far removed from now that it shocks me when I revisit them. However, the changes can sometimes be so imperceptible that we don't notice them on a day-to-day basis, so it is very helpful to have a record of your own personal transformation.

Work through the Quantum Qualities in the order that they are presented in this book. They are progressive with the power building through the different sections. None of them is more important than the next, yet they are magically linked to enhance your evolution.

In each of the Quantum Qualities there will be the following:

- **An Exercise**
- **A Meditation**
- **A Tip From Jo!**
- **A Reflection**
- **Questions and Answers**

This interactive programme sits beautifully alongside the Quantum Sobriety online programme, which you may like to join and where you receive the meditations in this book (and many more) already recorded for ease and the tasks emailed to you. You also have the chance for Q&As in the form of a monthly live webinar, weekly livestream trainings, support from the QS Guides; who have all been through the programme and have at least nine months of sobriety, and a very lively forum with discussions between like-minded, open-minded, non-judgemental individuals all making friends with their Quantum Superpower. If you do not want to be part of this community you can still purchase similar recorded meditations. Details are at the end of the book.

Quantum Quality One
Awareness

*'Insanity: doing the same thing over and over again
and expecting different results'*
Albert Einstein

It all begins with Awareness. We have to know where we
are, or where we are coming from, to be able to decipher
where we need to go; it's taking stock, looking around,
and understanding how our limiting beliefs have led us to
the life we are experiencing, *without guilt.*

How were we supposed to know all of this if our parents
also didn't know so *couldn't* teach us, and nobody at
school knew either so they *couldn't* educate us in the
subject of 'self enquiry'. So there can be no guilt, no self-
flagellation, no blame.

We are the lucky ones to be learning this information
now, and we are in the minority, for most are soldiering
on unknowingly on the treadmill of normality.

So look around, what do you see? What's good in your
life? What do you want to change? Where do you want to
go?

Separation
We are going to start off switching roles and become the
observer of our lives. By stepping back and taking a look

at our world *as an outsider*, rather than being right in the middle caught up in the details, we will begin to see things differently.

If all around us there are waves of potentials just waiting for our attention, then *what* are you choosing? Science gives us these possibilities but it cannot do anything about them, it is *only* an observer, only YOU, can turn that potential into an actual experience. I know that I have bumbled through life not realising that I am creating every single occurrence, every single thought, every single projection that I have. Going around and around in circles living the same life day in and day out, especially when I have been heavily addicted to substances or behaviours.

Quantum Meditation
It's time to extract ourselves from the slavery of our lives and begin to see everything from a new perspective; separating ourselves from our thoughts, actions, beliefs, attitudes, dramas and addictions.

We begin to open the void between who we've always been and who we have the potential to become, tentatively taking the first few steps in this new world. We will begin getting some perspective with the **Ocean Meditation** and start the process of 'letting go', for if we can learn to let go of thoughts as they pass through the mind in meditation then we can take this quality from our 'formal' (meditation) practice to the 'informal' (rest of our life) experience.

And this is the recurring theme throughout this approach… that we learn to do something in the container which is the meditative state, get so good at it there, that it naturally spills out over the edge and into the pool which is the rest of our lives. THIS is why we meditate. This is the beauty of it, the power of it, how it will transform our lives from the inside out.

We Are Not Our Thoughts
Thoughts are just things that pass through our minds, and can differ on the same subject depending on our mood. Just think how you feel about your kids or family day-to-day; it can be quite varied, especially if we are tired or hungover.

So we disentangle ourselves from our thoughts and allow them to pass through, one by one, letting them go, over and over again.

This is the theme for our first meditation, finding the separation and ultimately discovering who you really are…

Meditation Preparation
- Where are you going to meditate? This is when we want to create a positive association with a quiet part of our home where we are most likely to be left alone. Meditate in the same place every day, so that this space becomes somewhere that you want to visit over and over again. Place a picture on the table or shelf of someone or something that inspires you and if not a picture then a phrase or mantra. Then light a candle and burn some incense. Maybe have fresh flowers in the room; whatever makes you feel relaxed. Ultimately this is going to become your sacred space and will help to 'anchor' your practice.
- Time of day is very important, with first thing in the morning before you have fully woken up being the absolute best time, or just before you

go to bed (more detail on this in Chapter 10, see p.163).

- If your mind is very busy and you are not listening to a recorded version of these meditations then you may want to play some soft peaceful music. It should have no words and no emotional connotations, as you do not want to get pulled off by it and have a conversation in your head about what happened last time you heard it. The best kind to purchase would be singing bowl music or the sound of the sea, rain or birds.

- Decide how long you are going to meditate for and set a timer so that you do not have to worry about it. In the beginning this only needs to be 5 or 10 minutes. The most important aspect here is that you are creating a new habit, a new pathway in the brain.

  IMPORTANT: If you feel all enthusiastic in the beginning and say, *'Right I'm really up for this and I'm going to meditate for 30 minutes'* and then you sit there twiddling your thumbs bored out of your mind, then you are going to send a BORED message to your brain *'meditation is boring',* plus release BORED chemicals into your body. It's not going to work! It's not sustainable! Believe me in my very classic addictive-nature way, I've tried it. The problem then is that you have created a negative association in the brain, and you don't want to meditate ever again.

  NB: the meditations on the online programme are between 20 and 30 minutes long, and are guided to lead you on a journey deep within yourself. Most members say they cannot believe how quickly the time goes.

- If you are not using the recordings get yourself a timer app (there are some great singing bowl ones) or use your phone. I always put my phone onto aeroplane mode so that I am not giving myself a zap of interference when I am connecting deeply with the quantum field.

- You will be building up your meditation for longer and longer periods over time, and only you will know when it's time to meditate for longer. Do not force anything.

- Once you have got yourself comfortable then try not to move unless you have to. However, it's important to be comfortable whilst meditating so if you need to move your leg during the time you've allotted yourself then you must do so, however, you want to make any movements *mindful* and *minimal*: Know you are going to move before you actually do so. We are tying to get as relaxed as possible so if you are in agony then you are not going to be very relaxed.

- Your posture should be in the paradoxical meditative state of aware yet relaxed (so should your mind); you are sitting tall with your back and shoulders forming a lifting T-structure of support, and the rest of your body is completely relaxed around this frame. If you can get your body to do this, then your mind will follow.

- You should always breath in AND out through your nose (unless specifically directed differently). The nose is designed for breathing, with the mouth being used for breathing only in an emergency (if you have a cold).

- Read through each meditation before you do it, or you could recite it (slowly and calmly, leaving gaps in between the sentences) into a smartphone so that you can listen back to it effortlessly with your eyes closed. (If you are a member of the online community you will get each of the meditations in this book, and more, emailed to you for ease.)

- Make sure you are not going to be disturbed. Turn you phone off (or put it onto aeroplane mode), close the door and let your family know you will be back in 5, 10, 20 or 30 minutes.
- Take off your watch (a watch has its own rhythm which is not the same as yours, and remember we want to connect to our own personal energy field).
- Take off your glasses when meditating as they distort your natural vision.

MEDITATION ONE: The Ocean Meditation
- Decide how long you are going to meditate for and set a timer so that you do not have to worry about it.
- Sit comfortably in either a chair or on a cushion on the floor.
- Rest your hands either in your lap, one on top of the other with both thumbs touching (Buddha style), or each hand resting on your knees with first fingers and thumbs together (a la yoga = chin mudra)
- Your back is super straight, against a wall is much comfier in the beginning until your back is strong enough to be away from the wall, or sitting in a straight-backed chair.
- Eyes are closed.

Become aware of your breath, noticing without judgement the length and quality. Notice how your body feels in its sitting position, again with no judgement. Already you are becoming the observer, the watcher, and now start to watch your thoughts as they pass through your mind like clouds.

Have you noticed how clouds don't stop in the sky? They are constantly moving, sometimes fast sometimes slow. See if you can decipher the space between you (consciousness) and your thoughts (things). Do this for the first few minutes at least (longer when doing an extended practice).

Then imagine that you are swimming in the ocean. It is warm and tropical, but don't worry if you cannot swim, as within our visualisations anything is possible and you can swim effortlessly. There is no struggle.

What does the water feel like, what is the temperature? What movement is there? What can you see around you and on the horizon? What is in the sky; blue sky or cloud formations? Can you taste or smell the water? What does it sound like as it moves against you? You are using your senses to make the visualisation as real as possible.

It's very pleasant and you lie on the surface of the water floating and enjoy how the water is supporting you. Sometimes life is like this, and we feel supported. Sometimes everything seems to go our way and life is easy, in flow, uncomplicated.

Then we notice that there is a storm coming in with the cloud building and the wind picking up. As the storm gets closer and closer the water gets a little choppy and there are spots of rain.

Then it is right on us and it is pouring with rain, strong wind, and the waves are high and crashing all around us. It's hard to stay afloat and we are furiously treading water. Sometimes life is like this: difficult; problematic; stressful, triggering and turbulent: but it is the same for all of us. We all experience times of loss, pain, hurt or ill health, whether we are addicted to something or not; it is the human condition.

So we are going to drop down underneath the surface of the water and descend down to where it is always quiet and peaceful. As we do so we get further and further away from the storm.

And don't worry we can breath under water in this visualisation!

As we get deeper and deeper we feel calmer and calmer. We are creating SPACE from us and the storm, SPACE between consciousness and thought. We are breaking down through the barrier between conscious and subconscious mind.

We reach the bottom and it is so quiet down here. This is where we are going to stay for the duration of our meditation whether that is just for a few minutes or longer.

Look up at the surface and see that the storm is still raging up there, BUT WE ARE NOT BEING AFFECTED BY IT DOWN HERE.

And the same thing is happening with our thoughts: they are still there just as the storm is, but we have moved our brain activity to a different part of the brain so that our thoughts are not pulling us towards them quite as strongly. It's like we can let them pass much more easily when we're down here.

Spend as long as you have down here enjoying the SPACE that you have created within yourself. And whatever is going on in your life at the moment can be represented by the storm: an addiction; a person; a job, etc.

Once your timer has sounded it is time to swim back up to the surface of the water. The storm has now passed. You return with a new sense of self and a deeper connection to who you really are. Once at the top let go of the visualisation and bring your hands to your chest in a prayer position. Look down towards your heart and

thank yourself for beginning this journey.
Congratulations! You just completed your first QS
meditation.

Overview
Physiologically what is happening in this meditation is
that we are moving brain activity from the right to the left
prefrontal cortex. As we leave the stress-prone right side
where we experience anger, anxiety and fear, we instead
stimulate the peaceful left side, where that beautiful
feeling of unity, contentment and love resides.

Don't forget that the more often we swing the pendulum
to the left, the plasticity of the brain will create new
connections so that we remain peaceful even outside
of our practice. The more we meditate the less life can
knock us down.

On the mind level we are dropping down into the
subconscious and into the 95% area in the diagram. We
move away from logic and reason, and instead connect
to our essence; where all of the answers to the questions
that we have reside.

Now that we have found some inner space, what did you notice was going on in your own personal 'storm'? What kind of thoughts were you having? Where did your mind want to go? And how easy did you find it to drop down into your subconscious mind? Remember to take notes of your on-going journey in your journal.

Bagua

From our new viewpoint post-meditation it is time to air our dirty laundry and get personal. We are about to look into all of the creases and crevices of all areas of our lives and make some decisions as to where we are going. I like to use the Chinese Bagua for this, which is a template used in the ancient art of Feng Shui which finds balance in one's home. Well, our lives are our homes so we can also use this model to find personal equilibrium.

The Bagua is broken down into nine areas, and by looking at each we create a balanced life with all areas being equally worked on.

Wealth	Reputation	Love
Health	Wellbeing	Family
Knowledge	Career	Spirituality

So let's break down each area and start to have a think about where we are right now and where we'd like to be, and remember there are no limits. We are harnessing our ANYTHING attitude.

Career:

Knowledge:

EXERCISE FIVE: **What Is The Plan?**
OK, in these same areas start to write where you want to
go. This time you can take your time, make yourself a cup
of tea, go for a walk, connect with your quantum friend
(the pure potentiality that is all around you) and then
come back refreshed and think about the future. Write
what your dream is: if you could have anything what
would it be? Expand your mind and open yourself up to
the limitless opportunities that are all around you for the
taking. Use more paper if it feels appropriate to do so.
However if you have absolutely no idea what to put in a
few or all sections do not worry, as this is exactly what
this book is all about; we are going to find the answers
within us once we have established a meditation practice.

Relationships:

Wealth:

Reputation:

Health:

Wellbeing:

Family:

Spirituality:

Career:

Knowledge:

Conclusion

Once you have completed the first meditation and these tasks you are going to have a much-improved idea of where you are at in this moment. It is imperative that we create awareness in all corners of our lives.

This may not have been an easy task, with difficult answers arising, but easy or not it has to be done if we are to progress to the next Quantum Quality. Awareness is the building block for everything else, and hopefully you now have a clearer picture of your situation. There will probably be one or two areas that need immediate attention with others requiring just a little fine-tuning. However, now that we know what we're dealing with hopefully you are full of enthusiasm to change your life forever.

REFLECTION: **Heartbeat**

I'd like you to make room in your journal for a 'reflection' section. At the end of each chapter I'm going to ask you a question, to which it's important that you write down your *immediate* response. It's so interesting to watch how our perceptions change from start to finish of this process, *but if you don't do it as you're reading the book it's not going to have an impact* so get organised now; maybe start your normal journalling from the front of the book and your reflections from the back.

Stop what you are doing and place one or both hands on your heart. You may like to do this when you are sitting or quickly lie down to do it. Can you feel your heart beating? If you can't, don't worry, it sometimes takes some time to gain access to the subtle beat. You may need to walk up the stairs to really get your heart pounding in your chest, and then place your hand there, close your eyes and see if you can picture what is going on internally; how blood is being pumped around the whole of your body from this point just underneath your hand/s. You may like to do this exercise after all strenuous activity to develop a beautiful new relationship with your heart.

Questions and Answers: **Awareness**

Q: You have said to sit in a chair or on the floor, but can I lie down?

A: I get asked this all of the time and I used to say to people that they could lie down on the floor, but they very often fell asleep! Sometimes they snored very loudly too! You are also creating a new habit and if you learn to meditate lying down then you will be making that physiological association with meditation. Plus have you *ever* seen Buddha meditating lying down?!

Q: I find it really difficult to visualise anything, is it still working?

A: Yes! Do your best. Some people find it very challenging to visualise and it will improve the more you try. But stay with the meditation 'story' as much as you can and 'see' it as clearly as possible; as long as you stay present and don't allow your mind to wander off anywhere then you are meditating. It will get easier the more you do it. And please don't worry as this is a very common occurrence in the beginning; the brain is being asked to do something new and may put up a bit of a fight until it gets used to the new command.

Q: I have trouble sleeping. Will meditation help?

A: Yes! Absolutely, and the Ocean Meditation is really great to visualise if you can't sleep as you are moving brain activity and deepening brain waves. Imagine that you are sinking into a very deep sleep as you move down towards the ocean floor.

Q: I am frightened of water after an accident when I was younger, and I don't think I will be able to relax in the Ocean Meditation.
A: Then don't do it if it is going to cause you stress. Concentrate instead on the clouds passing through the sky, noticing how much distance there is between you and them. Sometimes there are no clouds in the sky and it is gorgeously sunny, and other times there is a huge storm with torrential rain, even thunder and lightning: that storm is your drama.

Time to move on to our next Quantum Quality.

Quantum Quality Two
Unlearning

*If we **know** that change is possible then we will find the motivation to stop the addictive cycle*

Now it is time to shift through the lifetime of conditioning that has enveloped you from birth. From the news that bombards us daily to the school we went to, there have been certain subliminal messages that have seeped to our very core that must be eradicated like weeds.

Up until now we have been a product of our environment, and we didn't know any different, but it is time to create the reality that we *choose* rather than the one we have been given thus far.

The Quantum Detox

With all withdrawal there is going to be an uncomfortable period. As we peel away the layers that have cocooned us and kept us from our truth, we are going to uncover raw wounds that we must tend to with love. Through this process I would advise you find yourself somebody that you can talk it through with, whether that be a therapist, specialist programme or support network (more about this in Part Three). It is exactly why I have set up the online programme so that no matter where in the world you are, there is always someone going through something similar to bounce ideas off and chat it through with. Finding a counsellor or similar may be more suitable for your personal needs and I talk about this in more detail in Part Three also.

For some of us it is going to be a detox from a substance as well as the emotional attachment that comes with it, while for others reading this it is going to be a lifetime of anger or (place your emotion in here) issues. Whatever is out of balance, whatever is being addressed, this initial stage is like pulling off a plaster: some will do it without batting an eyelid, whilst others will feel the pain of every single hair as it releases from the glue. We just don't know how we are going to cope until we start.

A Can Of Worms
It is highly possible that when we do begin to do these meditations and work with our subconscious mind, that we uncover what is *really* going on. There is always a reason behind our addiction and here is your WARNING: things could get hairy as we fight our way through the woods, but there is a beautiful meadow just beyond the brambles and this amazing place is waiting for *you*.

The Three Choices: Before, During and After a Trigger
We have three stages towards an action, giving us THREE opportunities to catch our addiction/emotion before it leads us into the very behaviour we are trying to eliminate:

1. BEFORE: the assessment / consideration / evaluation / judgement
2. DURING: the impulse / desire / urge / compulsion / itch
3. AFTER: the action

In the beginning we need to be prepared for when we do experience a trigger, to find the *inner space* we discovered during the Ocean Meditation, and this is exactly what the next meditation will arm us with. Ultimately this is how we are going to find freedom; by continuingly increasing the gap between what is creating so much destruction in our lives and the life we have the potential of realising.

Right now our propensity to what we've always done is automatic, *there is NO gap*; we just do it without any thought, so we need to bring the awareness that we first started to connect with in the previous chapter to the *trigger zone.*

When we can access this space within there is only connection to our essence, and that part of us does not want to stuff emotions down with food, feel angry, numbed out with alcohol or high on drugs; because that takes us *away* from who we really are.

We want to move *away* from what is out of balance;
We want to move *towards* who we want to become.
Therefore:
The gap *increases* from who we were;
The gap *decreases* to who we are becoming.

The Magical Gap
It is this 'gap' which fuels our Quantum Superpower and we must work daily to connect to it. If we do it is like inviting magic into our lives. Buddhism calls it 'emptiness' which confuses most people, for who wants to feel empty? But in fact what emptiness really denotes is *oneness;* connection to self like you've never known it before. Total and utter peace is achieved. This is the promise of the Quantum Superpower. This is what I experience on a daily basis and it has been born purely out of meditation.

I searched for so many years for this feeling, as from the earliest age I *knew* subliminally that it was achievable. But in a suburban town in Essex (on the outskirts of London) in the 1980s and 1990s the only answers I found were in the highs of drugs and later on through the disconnection of alcohol. In the beginning these highs were satisfactory but I soon realised that this was not in fact what I was looking for, and I began the long search to find the magical gap that I now experience as a permanent state.

It hasn't happened overnight but I have proved that it is possible over the course of a number of years: to truly and fully become free (and bear in mind that I have had to discover this myself, rather than read and learn the process from a book). So again I confirm that even though this journey may be a long one, others have already reached the shore and are enjoying the luscious fruits of their labour; there are many in the QS community who are also experiencing freedom.

Sit on your cushion and meditate everyday. In the words of one of my teachers:

'Just practise.'
Lama Yeshe Rinpoche

Mind Muscle
The more we practise the easier it is going to be, and this is where creating a new habit of meditation is going to link in perfectly with your new emotional habits. We've learnt in earlier chapters how we create new pathways in the brain and can break away from unwanted ones, and by making the commitment to meditate everyday we are already starting to use the brain in a different way;

it's waking up to the idea of change as we exercise the muscle and make it strong.

Marathon Mind

If we decide we are going to run a marathon we know we are going to have to make a plan to train for it, nobody can run a marathon successfully without preparation. In the exact same way we are now training for the rest of our lives; nothing is the same now. We've taken on a new challenge and are, therefore, in uncharted water; we've never been here before and it may be scary at times.

New Chemical Signature

What we are going to start to notice is that the gap between impulse and action becomes bigger: we are reacting less and less where in the past we did so without even thinking. We suddenly realise that it doesn't have to be as it's been for what seems like forever; it can be different, better. BUT it is going to take repetition for this to become our new normal. Our brain is changing with *every single* decision that we make; positive or negative, it is our responsibility and nobody can do this for us. So in this way we are creating a brand new chemical signature which means we begin to feel and act very differently.

MEDITATION TWO: The Trigger Meditation
- Decide how long you are going to meditate for and set a timer so that you do not have to worry about when to finish.
- Sit comfortably in either a chair or on a cushion on the floor.
- Rest your hands either in your lap, one on top of the other with both thumbs touching (Buddha style), or each hand resting on your knees with

---

first fingers and thumbs together (a la yoga = chin mudra).
- Your back is super straight, against the wall or against the back of a straight-backed chair.
- Eyes are closed.

Become aware of your breathing and begin to follow it in and out of your body. Become the observer of your thoughts as they pass through your mind. Are they thoughts of the past? Or from the future? Begin to notice what *kind* of thoughts you're having. Planning? Worrying? Reminiscing? Are they pulling you in? Do they demand your attention? Can you let them go?

Now imagine that you are peeling off an outer layer which contains all of the stress that you are experiencing in life at the moment. You may want to pick this outer skin up, roll it into a ball and throw it away, as you no longer require this part of you. This is the old you, the conditioned you. The you that is a product of your environment.

Once you take off this outer coat you may feel a little exposed and unsure of yourself, or you may feel instantly liberated.

Keep coming back to your breath, returning to the present moment, pulling the mind back from wherever it just wandered off to. **This is the main meditation instruction**: *returning to the present moment over and over again.*

When your mind feels settled imagine walking down a staircase, each step taking you down further into your subconscious mind. What does the staircase look like? Is it wide? Narrow? Wooden or metal? Is there a light on, or a window? Try to get as many details as possible, but if you find visualisation difficult do not worry; do your best because it's working anyway. *Every step down is taking you deeper into your subconscious mind.*

When you get to the bottom of the stairs there is a corridor with many doors on either side. Walk down the corridor until you get to a door with a sign on it saying 'Conference Room'. Walk in and sit down at the table inside. On one side of you your higher self is going to come in and sit at the table, next to you. They may take physical form or be more like a spirit or mass of energy. You may recognise them or maybe not.

When you are doing these visual meditations there are no wrong or right answers; everyone is going to have a different experience and you will have a different experience each time you do the same meditation.

On the other side your teachers, guides, animal healers and spirits are going to come in. Perhaps there are people who are still alive here and also some who have already passed over. There may be one or four or 10 or 100 people present, again each time you do this meditation you will see something/someone different. Try not to project what you *think* you are going to experience. You feel extremely safe and loved in this room; these are your people. They love you and want the very best for you.

Now take out your addiction and put it on the table. What does it look like? Sound like? Taste like? Is it rough or smooth? What colour is it? You are not your addiction; it is separate from you and does not define you. And because this book has found its way to you it means that you are ready to step out of your addiction and up to a higher potential for yourself. Get to know your addiction as it sits on the table, completely separate to you, seeing it differently now because it has less power over you. Spend as much time as you need to here, then when you feel ready (or time is running out) put your addiction back inside you. What does it feel like to have it be part of you again? Can you tolerate it?

And then take it back out again onto the table, as much of it as you possibly can although this is going to be an on-going process and I recommend you do this meditation everyday for a month. This time one of your guides who is in the room with you is going to take whatever is on the table away and remove it completely; you never have to have it as part of you again, *if this is what you choose*.

Now someone who is in the conference room is going to give you a gift. You may know what it is or not, it doesn't matter; just accept what is being offered, knowing that it is exactly what you need in this moment and thank everyone. It's time to leave now and you say goodbye and leave the room, walk back along the corridor and up the stairs. As you walk up the stairs you connect the different parts of your mind: subconscious and conscious now working *together* as you become super-conscious. Once at the top, walk over to a waterfall and sit underneath it. The water is going to enter the top of your head and imagine higher energies filling you up and giving you whatever is essential for you right now. Feel refreshed, replenished, energised and excited about the future.

Come back to your breath again and notice how you feel at the end of the meditation compared to the beginning. What's changed? Do you feel different?

Overview

The power of this meditation is not to be underestimated. For the first time ever we may feel able to disconnect from the drama and control that our addiction has had over us, however many years we've been playing out this story. There have been many reports that doing this meditation just once has created such a new awareness of someone's addiction that they have stopped drinking / drugging / bingeing effortlessly in that moment.

Use It

Each time you get triggered to eat something, drink something or snort something, use this technique; take the feeling *out* of you and examine it. Know that it is not intrinsically a part of you, and that the more you question its existence the less power it can have over you.

So the instruction is to do this meditation every day for a month. Thirty minutes each day is optimum but you can practice for less if time is an issue. Then as you get used to doing it daily, you can call upon it in an instant when you need to; when you are in the midst of a major trigger.

For most when I say put the addiction back inside them after they have already taken it out, they are appalled by the suggestion and do not want to, or even cannot force it back inside. When you see it's true nature why would you choose to hold on to what is destroying you?

I have done this meditation myself hundreds of times after being taught it by the Chocolate Shaman*, and each time it is different. I don't want to tell you about my own experiences as you may take these ideas and project them into your own meditation experience but rest assured there have been some very interesting, weird, wonderful and powerful visuals!

Make a note of your own experience the first time you do this meditation, and then in subsequent repetitions of it. Notice how the practice changes day to day.

* I talk about the Chocolate Shaman in more detail in Part Three.

Tip!
I have been meditating for a very long time and over the years I've experienced all sorts of tightness in my body whilst meditating. Stick with it and these will all pass with time; it is your ego putting up a fuss and not wanting to settle.

Sometimes I have an urge to crack my neck and roll my head around to stretch it. What this means is you have gone into your conscious mind '*Am I doing this right?*', '*Wonder what's for dinner?*', '*Why can't I visualise the staircase?*', instead of being deep in your subconscious. So let go of the voice that wants to wake you up (ego) and walk back down the stairs into the deepest parts of you.

EXERCISE SIX: Who Is Influencing You?
We are blitzed with a media shower of wars, government scandals, atrocities and celebrity gossip. All of this negative input is being processed by your brain and stored in your memory, and if you allow it in it will keep you thinking small, scared and conditioned.

Being dictated to by our outside environment is the *opposite* of connecting to our inner voice, which is the only place that we find peace. After all have you ever seen happy stories being regularly shown in the headlines? Newspapers, magazines and TV sell what's shocking, not what's uplifting, and it's time to purge being drawn in by these mediums.

This exercise is about taking a look at the following list, and making a note of what kinds of publications you read and which TV programmes you view. Are you being inspired when you turn the TV on or demotivated? Are you uplifted when you read the paper or sent sinking into a depression?

- Newspapers: which one: how frequent
- Magazines: which ones: how frequent
- News on TV: how frequent
- Soaps on TV: which ones: how frequent
- Reality TV shows: which ones: how frequent
- Movies: which type: how frequent

As you can see there are a whole host of demons just waiting to get their claws into you. I don't read anything other than inspiring books/magazines but if I happen to pick up a newspaper or trashy magazine (not very often admittedly but I do on occasion) I am shocked at how easily I am pulled in, and how difficult it is to pull myself back out.

Conclusion

Today is the first day of the rest of your life, the past has been energetically released and it's now up to you what you bring into it. Choose wisely! Because up until now you have allowed what others have decided is in your best interest and it's time to make a stand, to make decisions based on your happiness. *Your* new life has just been born.

REFLECTION 1: **How Did You Do?**

Sometimes when we write things down we see them in a whole new light. The above exercise may have been shocking to you as you realise just how much of your time is taken up with what the media feeds you. I once calculated my TV viewing in a year and was shocked at all the time I had wasted. For the majority of it I was hungover and unable to leave my home. The crazy thing is that at the time I was living in Thailand and if I hadn't been sat in front of the telly I could have been on the beach and swimming in the beautiful ocean.

REFLECTION 2: **What Do You Believe About Love?**

Jot down in your journal what beliefs you hold around love, being loved and self-love. We are going to be coming on to this subject in much more detail in the next chapter, so just before we get there make a note of where you are *now* around the subject. It's wonderful to keep having these points of reference on your journey.

Questions and Answers: **Unlearning**

Q: Are you saying that we shouldn't ever read a newspaper again?

A: Yes and no. For me the perfect balance is having the news on a couple of times a week to keep abreast of current affairs. I want to know the basic headlines but I won't watch the whole programme, which is where you get sucked in to the details.

Q: Some really scary stuff comes out onto the table in the conference room and I am feeling a little overwhelmed with it all.

A: Firstly just think how much better it is to have that scary stuff out on the table rather than inside you. Make sure you get yourself over to the waterfall and fill yourself up with the higher energies; this is a vital part of the meditation exercise, as the trigger bit can be extremely intense and must be balanced out. Also you will be processing this meditation for quite a few hours after you've done it, so look after yourself.

Secondly I think it would be very helpful to get support around this; talk to a counsellor, therapist or someone in the QS community. You can connect with our global team anytime.

Q: I really like the idea of the Trigger Meditation but I am finding it difficult to even get down the stairs! What's going on?

A: This is actually really good news. The struggle means that your mind *knows* that something is about to change and is resisting. Don't push yourself too hard though. Keep trying to go down and one day you will be able to, or maybe your higher self or one of your guides could come out of the conference room and come up to get you? Just a suggestion! It's your meditation.

Time to move on to our next Quantum Quality....

Quantum Quality Three
Forgiveness And Love

*We are containers of compassion as we channel it to others, and of
course the vessel is touched by what is contained therein*

Now that we are detoxing from the past we must forgive
ourselves, and others, for past actions. Without doing this
we can never fully let go of who we were, to be able to
embrace the fullness of who we are to become. The first
three Quantum Qualities are steeped in 'letting go' energy
and form the ground or soil for what we are going to
start building in the next stages.

A Line In The Sand
We weren't to know how it was going to turn out, we
didn't get all of the information, but we have it now so it's
time to draw a line in the sand. This is that moment.

Deeply forgive yourself and replace any remnants of
guilt or blame with love. You are here now and that is all

that matters, guilt will only hold you back, bind you to the past and who you used to be and fill your head with negative chatter.

The Guilt Game
This is a huge point and one that a lot of people get stuck on. Once we realise that everything that we are experiencing has come from our own making, so many people feel *worse* about themselves and push these teachings away. But the point is that *we didn't know* what we were doing so we mustn't blame ourselves. This is where drawing a line in the sand is so important, take THIS MOMENT as the first moment of the rest of your life, and *start now*. All that matters is what happens from this point. And things will not change immediately as what we are experiencing today is a result of what we created yesterday, and we have to wait until tomorrow for today's creations to manifest. Please do not get caught up in the guilt game. Take responsibility from now, pledge to yourself that you will do the best that you possibly can. Nobody can ask more of you than that.

Forgiving Others
What may have come up for you already, especially in the Trigger Meditation are difficult situations with others. There may well be a strained relationship with your parents or siblings, or an incident in your past that has caused you to press the self-destruct button. The bingeing on drugs, food or anything else is usually the result of something much deeper going on, so there could well be individuals with whom you are not at peace. Forgiving yourself comes *first* as you must 'be the change' but the next step is moving the feeling outwards and there are a few ways you can do this.

EXERCISE SEVEN: **Forgiving Others**

If you feel you are able to speak to the person directly, brilliant, as this will be the quickest way of resolving bad feelings. But for most this will not sit comfortably, especially if we feel the person has done us wrong. In this instance the very first step would be to write them a letter, even if you have no intention of sending it. This exercise is primarily for *you* so you can be at ease with the situation. Write the letter, *exactly* how you feel in this moment, and notice if your emotions have altered. Just doing this alone can bring about huge changes, whether you actually send the letter or speak to the person or not. Can you see that you have taken the situation OUT of yourself (like taking your addiction out and putting it on the conference room table), so that you can gain insight into it not being yours at all.

Time For Self-Love

Right here this book shifts again, as when we forgive and let go of the past we make more space for LOVE. There is only love or fear. The choice is yours which kind of life you want, but when you fill your heart with love the ONLY emotion that the quantum field can return to you is love. Of all the waves of possibilities available, when you send out love then it *has* to be love that comes back.

So our primary job must be to generate love and compassion daily. This then becomes our main priority and seeing ourselves in others is the easiest way I've found of developing this quality.

Ultimately every single being on the planet *(not just humans)* wants to be healthy and happy. We have so much in common yet sometimes it feels like we are poles apart. So how do we feel kinship with complete strangers?

This meditation comes in two halves; the first being about forgiveness and the second generating compassion for self and others. Bring in to the forgiveness section a different situation/person/addiction/experience each time, eventually (but not all at once) working through all that needs healing and resolving.

MEDITATION THREE: Forgiveness And Compassion

- Decide how long you are going to meditate for and set a timer so that you do not have to worry.
- Sit comfortably in either a chair or on a cushion on the floor.
- Rest your hands either in your lap or each hand resting on your knees with first fingers and thumbs together.
- Your back is super straight, against the wall or against the back of a straight-backed chair.
- Eyes are closed.

Become aware of your breathing as it enters and leaves your body and step back from your thoughts, becoming the watcher of them rather than being comprised of them. Spend a couple of minutes here stabilising your mind. The more regularly you meditate the easier this is going to become.

Decide what you are going to work with today and what you would like to forgive. Bring this person/situation out in front of you at heart level. Then notice that there is a thread that joins you, like an umbilical cord, and until you are ready to let this person or situation go you are feeding it through the connection. You may notice smaller, less dense threads between the two of you as well; these will be easier to break. Say thank you to this situation/addiction/experience for all that it has shown you and then tell it that you are ready to move on. Cut all of the cords that connect you to each other, one by one. As the last one is severed the situation/person/addiction begins to float away from you, like a leaf in the breeze. Send it love as it goes; it made you stronger, it allowed you to turn inward and begin to question your life, and recognise that you have become a better person because of it. Watch as it gets smaller and smaller on the horizon, and then it is gone.

Now bring your attention to your heart and begin to generate the feeling of love. If this is difficult then think of somebody that you love very much, and start to direct the love towards yourself. Some people will find this very difficult as they have never 'loved' themselves before and it is an alien concept to them but give it a go; it will get easier with time. Love the fact that you are meditating right now. Love the fact that you want to be a better person. See if you can spread this feeling of love and compassion to the whole of you.

Then take this love and compassion out to the people that you love dearly in your life. Shower them with pure unconditional love. Stay with them for a few minutes, and then expand your field of attention to your immediate family, then to your extended family. Stay here for a while. Now you are generating even more love to encompass the people that live close by to you; your neighbours; village folk; the people that you see in the supermarket. Whether you know them very well or hardly at all it doesn't matter, you are scattering love and compassion widely.

Next we are widening our vision and sending love and compassion to everyone in our county/state/district. Of course we do not know these people but they have the same struggles, problems and dilemmas as us. They too want to be happy, successful and abundant.

Time now to increase the sharing of love and compassion even further to the whole of our country. We all share the same leader, policies, economic climate as each other; we have so much in common but we will never meet these people in our lifetime. Nevertheless they need our love right now. Magnify this energy even more as we cover the whole of our continent and then the entire planet. Can you picture the earth in your mind's eye and sprinkle it with love, wishing that every single person, animal, bird, reptile, fish and insect has received a piece of your heart? Then take this feeling to the whole universe; our solar system and beyond, whatever is out there, whatever you believe or are unsure about. Send love anyway just in case. Hopefully you should by now be feeling so full of love that you might burst. Stay here in this beautiful moment for as long as you can, holding the vision in your mind.

Then start to bring your energy back again to our solar system, then back to our planet, your continent, your country, your county/state/district, your town/village, neighbours, extended family, immediate family, loved ones and then finally back to you. All of that love that you just sent out to the whole universe is now just for *you*, because you deserve that much love. Stay in this vibration of magnified love for as long as you can.

And lastly we are going to make this even more of a quantum meditation by giving love to our past self and our future self as well as our present self. Shower love to the situation/person that you began this meditation with. Send love out into all future situations that you will find yourself in so that it will meet you when you arrive. And stay with this love and compassion for as long as you have left in your meditation, and afterwards see if you can maintain the feeling all day, evening, week, month, year, forever if that is possible.

Overview

What is happening here is that as soon as you let go of a difficult situation/relationship there is a vacuum, which you are filling with love, and when you send love out to someone else it is filling YOU up first. This happens automatically but we are usually not aware of it, so when you are conscious of this love rippling through your body then your brain communicates it to your body and every single cell begins to bathe in it too. Your whole being vibrates with love and remember when we are experiencing love on the inside we are asking for love to manifest on the outside in the form of people, experiences, places, gifts etc.

We are softening to others, even strangers or people that we don't like. We become gentle, tender, forgiving, undemanding and easy to be around. We start to see the good in people rather than just the annoying tendencies that once we would have focused on.

Scientific Viewpoint

There has been much study of the effects on the brain specifically from meditating on compassion, showing a marked leftward shift in the prefrontal cortex where we know feelings of happiness and contentment are born. The results are like creating an extremely good mood. It has now also been proved that by having concern for another's welfare, we create a greater state of wellbeing within ourselves.

Buddhist Viewpoint

I remember reading one of the Dalai Lama's books a number of years ago where he called himself and others like him who do a lot of compassion practice the '*selfish Buddhas*' because he knows that by doing this practice first he is the receiver of the benefit before it radiates outwards to everybody else. We are containers of compassion as we channel it to others, and of course the vessel is touched by what is contained therein.

> '*I feel from my own experience that when I practice compassion there is an immediate direct benefit to myself, not for others. By practicing compassion, I get 100% benefit, while the benefit to others may be 50%. So the main motivation for the practice of compassion is self-interest.*
> *I find that as soon as some kind of sense of caring or concern increases in my heart, this brings me more inner strength. The result: I feel less fear, more happiness. There are some problems here and there? Okay, no matter. If there is shocking news, sad news, I may be uncomfortable for a few seconds, but then I recover very swiftly and there is peace again. To conclude I think the practice of compassion is like a medication that restores serenity when one is very agitated, the great tranquilizer is compassion.*'
> HH Dalai Lama

Compassion is a natural emotion and easy to generate. Just thinking of complete strangers who have been in an accident or are living in a harsh part of the world instantly pulls at our heart strings and begins the process of compassion production; and just look at how communities/nations pull together after a natural disaster.

However, in the beginning it may feel contrived. As with the whole of the Quantum Sobriety programme we are changing the brain, so it takes repetition for a potentially unnatural emotion (compassion) to first become familiar, then arise easily, to taking no effort at all. That takes practice and is my own personal experience of compassion, which was almost alien to me at the beginning of my spiritual journey.

Ultimately when we have moved through the stages in this book, released our negative and destructive emotions and become free, we then open up so much space for helping others. Compassion arises naturally and is shared with others automatically. You get to the stage where you do not even have to think about it; it becomes second nature.

Tip! Meditation As Self-Compassion
As you have seen already meditation is the fast track route to a happier life; there is no other activity that has so much potential to create abundance, overcome addiction, and quite literally pull the very best of you to the surface. But it takes a commitment for it to become your new normal, and this is my advice for creating a strong daily practice...

Meditation – *Just 5 Minutes Will Do*
The daily practice that you have hopefully established by now is the quick perspective fix that will keep you on track. Ideally you are going to be doing this a few times per day, to check back in regularly and remain balanced throughout the day. In a perfect world you will be doing this first thing in the morning, at lunchtime/afternoon and in the evening.

Classes – *Going Deeper*
I also recommend you build your practice up with some bigger chunks of meditation. Going to a class or listening to a recording for 30 minutes is going to speed up the process. Remember that the more meditation you do the quicker you are going to start seeing the external changes. It's great to be part of a group whether that is in person or online, giving you access to a teacher who can answer your specific questions and guide you as you progress. Shop around and try a few out. Which teacher speaks your language? You must feel some sort of connection plus the teacher must be living what they are teaching themselves.

Into Retreat – *The Luxury Of A Whole Weekend (or more)*
There is great beauty in taking yourself away from your 'normal' world and spending time with people who are also on the journey towards freedom. At home there are expectations, judgements, appointments, time constraints, stress around money and arguments.

We need to regularly surround ourselves with people who are already where we would like to be, so that we are constantly up-levelling ourselves rather than staying the same. We expand when we're out of our comfort zone; this is where change is possible, and if we place ourselves in a retreat environment we have so much time to do the inner work, *and also we don't have to worry about cooking dinner!*

It is here where we can access even more inner space, it's like everything slows down and we can see what is really going on. Without the deadlines, bills to pay, kids to get off to school there is room to think; to shift; to transform.

'What makes me happy?'
'What job do I really want to do?'
'What is my purpose?'

These are questions that we should all be asking ourselves all of the time. They are a priority, but most of the time we are far too stressed to be pondering such 'trivia'. Take yourself to a place where there is no resistance, a sacred space that will hold and nurture your growth. You will literally feel yourself unwrap and in this process unmask what you usually show to the world, and allow yourself to become who you *really* are.

Retreating At Home
For some it is going to be impossible to get away from everyday life, although I would still urge you to do so even if it is just for one day twice a year. This is a good exercise for us all to do anyway once a month:
Look at your diary/calendar and find a day that looks empty, if you have children then we are looking at the days that they are very busy and not at home. This is going to be your 'Home-treat', and you are *only* going to do things that you love and make you feel amazing. This is a day off, a treat, filled with wonderful activities and you are going to feel divine afterwards.

EXERCISE EIGHT: What Makes You Feel Relaxed?
Sometimes called 'self-care', I want you to list all of the things that make you feel amazing! I am going to give you some examples:

Long hot bath • Go for a walk • Spa day
Write your journal • Have a nap • Listen to music
Read a book • Massage

Overview

Why wouldn't you treat yourself in this way? Why do you not deserve the pleasures that you love? And *at least* once a month!

Think about when you are sitting on a plane listening to the safety announcement. We know that we have to put our own oxygen mask on first *so that* we can then look after everybody else. We are no good to anyone if we haven't first taken care of ourselves; this is one of the biggest mistakes we make. And this especially applies to women who take care of the home, their husband, the kids and then wonder why they are so exhausted that they haven't got the energy for an argument, let alone a normal conversation. It's all back to front. If this same woman had spent the day looking after herself before her family came home then she would feel relaxed, open and available. Can you see/understand the difference?

The Unexpected Payback

As soon as we begin to take care of ourselves our energy changes, and those in our lives begin to notice even if they can't quite put their finger on what's different. Because we have begun to love ourselves, others get the green light to love us more too and we begin to notice our friends and families mirroring our own new behaviour back to us.

REFLECTION: **How Does That Extra Love Feel?**
What has this chapter (and the meditation if you've already done it) made you feel like? Are you willing to take a look at 'self-love' and have a go at 'loving' yourself? Is this a new concept? Are you going to commit to a daily ritual of at least one enjoyable activity that you listed in the exercise? Can you feel your heart expanding?

Tip!

I remember when I started my meditation journey and was really struggling with it. Twenty minutes seemed like AGES. Then I would visit the monastery in Scotland where their sessions were an hour long, and it seemed to me to go on for HOURS! I would get fidgety, my back hurt, I was hungry, my neck hurt, what was for lunch? My jaw ached, an itch, my legs have gone numb...

What happened when I forced myself to sit through these long sessions was that it put me off practising altogether. I noticed a pattern that after I'd visited the monastery my own personal practice then diminished sometimes to nothing for months. So I cannot emphasise enough the importance of biting off *small* manageable chunks in the beginning. Don't scare yourself off because once you get out of the habit of meditating it can sometimes be difficult to get back in.

Now I am in a position that I get to the hour-long sessions earlier so that I can do *more* than 60 minutes, because it is no longer enough. That is what happens when you build your practice up sensibly; it becomes such an integral part of your life that you make time for it, get up earlier so that you can do it; it becomes like your best friend.

Questions and Answers: **Forgiveness And Love**

Q: I have a really difficult relationship with my mother and to be frank I just do not want to forgive her for what she has done to me, and others. How do I get past this?
A: Some people do terrible things to others but *they* are also a product of *their* environment and I wonder if their behaviour would be deemed 'normal' as they were

growing up? There are so many factors for each situation, and what is important here is how *you* are feeling. Write the letter in exercise seven and see if by getting your emotions out of yourself and on paper you feel a little lighter around the situation. It may never resolve itself entirely, especially if the person in question doesn't have the capacity to see they need to change; you can't do this for somebody else, but you can learn how to heal the wound. You may never forgive your mother to her face but behind closed doors come to some level of forgiveness of the situation, but never do anything that makes you feel uncomfortable. Begin to love yourself by committing to a routine of self-care and watch as others start to notice and initiate treating you better too.

Q: I've done some truly awful things when drunk and hurt so many people. Where do I start to mend my broken life?
A: Congratulations – you have already started; having the clarity that you no longer want to be where you are now is massive. You must open yourself up first, heal the wound that you uncover, and then build a new reality from the ruins. The thing is these ruins form fine fertile ground for an amazing new life and you are already well on the way to creating it.

Q: Do I have to be a Buddhist to do the compassion meditation?
A: Absolutely not. It is a meditation about love and altruism, and all faiths practice that.

Time to move on to our next Quantum Quality.

Quantum Quality Four
Acceptance

The heaviness of the past is no longer pulling you back and dragging you under, you are somewhere new

This chapter is about being in a neutral place, a level playing field. We've removed the plaster and observed what's festering underneath then forgiven everything that's happened in our lives that led to this wounding, *covering it instead with love.*

Once we have done this we arrive at Acceptance: of who we are; of why life is like it is; and the fact that we are in the driver's seat. We've now adjusted our set-point and are beginning to see things differently, that it's not doom and gloom any longer.

We are teetering into an unknown world, poking our head out of a door that we've only allowed open a fraction, and looking into this strange new place. No longer do we automatically think the worst; we've begun to see and believe that everything is going to be ok.

Zero Point

This is probably your first few steps out onto the quantum, and into the vast void of pure potentiality. In Acceptance you are having a *neutral* experience, sometimes talked about as the Zero Point: when the heaviness of the past is no longer pulling you back and dragging you under. Now with that weight gone from your shoulders you are somewhere new, standing on the edge of your old life and realising that there really *is* more. You have read about it in books, heard people talk about it, but never really known that it existed...until now.

Or perhaps you have had a taste of it before? But you only touched in on it for a second, then it was gone, and you start to hesitate; was it really there? Are you going mad?

I remember when I first began to experience the Zero Point. I had such a strong reaction because it was so different from anything that I'd ever experienced before (without drugs), that I really doubted myself. And it only came infrequently as I didn't understand it or know how to use it. No one around me seemed to know what the hell I was on about, so it became my secret. At the time I had just got into yoga and meditation and was reading as many self-help books as I could, but it was the mid-1990s and no one was talking about quantum physics back then.

I can't tell you what a relief it is finally to have the scientific knowledge to explain what I have been feeling for over 20 years, and to have science back up everything that I've experienced spiritually. And it was at that moment when everything became so clear to me that I knew I had to share the knowledge.

EXERCISE NINE: The Zero Point
For this exercise think about what takes you to the Zero Point, other than meditation. When do you feel really at peace with yourself? And then list the activities in your

journal. Here are some examples:

Go for a walk • Have a massage • Write/Journal
Sing • Exercise • Dance • Paint • Gardening

You want to be doing one of these things everyday *as well as meditating*; whatever gets you to the place of neutrality.

Time To 'Be'

So we now shift again, and the quantum qualities become less about *'doing'* something and more about *'being'*, with us being able to accept our life, our lessons, our struggles and our path just as it is.

I can see that *everything* that has happened in my life was preparing me for this very moment, for the writing of this book and sharing of my experience. Of course back then, when I was being called a vile four-letter word everyday by the man who was supposed to be in love with me, or when I woke up with the hangover from hell, I didn't see it that way. It was only afterwards on reflection that I can see each experience has been a layer of understanding that led me ultimately to the knowledge of how to be happy.

If I had known all of this back then I wouldn't have had to feel that half my life I've been stuck in quicksand, but I also know that it is *because* of all of that 'stuff' that I now have a reference point; I know how bad it can get, how we can fight against life, against our feelings; and against our intuition.

It is these difficulties that make us and we should not be ashamed of them. I get so many emails from people who read my blogs and cannot believe I am so open about alcohol and drug addiction, my bankruptcy, abusive relationships and more. But I believe that all of these things happened to me SO THAT I can help others across the lake of despair to the shore of hope, courage and optimism. I swam it and nearly drowned but this book is a boat that will lead you safely to the coastline. However, you still need to get in the boat, and put on your lifejacket, as the journey may be quite turbulent yet.

If you have had an addiction to something before and tried to give it up a number of times before you finally were successful then you will already have some insight into what this book is about. Mind-set is everything, and when I look back to my first few attempts of giving up cigarettes it was SO difficult. I couldn't do it. I lasted a day and then I was again puffing away on those evil sticks of dis-ease. But then when I did ultimately smoke my last one, when I had made the decision that I didn't want to do this anymore, it was EASY. Now the cigarettes were exactly the same brand, they hadn't changed, BUT I HAD. I was viewing them in a different way, my brain had changed (I didn't fully understand it at the time), and I let go of the struggle and accepted my new way of being.

Everything Changes
With everything in life constantly changing we can either go with the flow of what is so natural or hold on tight and resist. In addiction we are blinkered, we cannot see another way; it has to be like it's always been. We resist change all the time and therefore push away the unlimited possibilities that are available to us.
Science tells us that the universe is constantly expanding = change.
Buddhism tells us exactly the same thing: we all get old;

we all will die; we all suffer. And the root of suffering is fear. But work on our fear, transform it, and we become liberated and experience peace. Nothing has changed externally, yet our perception has changed and we can now see clearly.

It's taken us a few chapters to get to this point where we are ready to let go and allow. Up until now we've been clinging on to the waters edge holding on for dear life, fingers bleeding from gripping so tightly and quite literally overwhelmed with fear. But now it's time to let go. Let the river carry you downstream, why have you been fighting for so long when it is much easier to go with the flow? The reason is its part of our conditioning to fight. We are told from a young age that:

'Life is difficult.'
'Money doesn't grow on trees.'
'You have to work hard and long hours to succeed.'
'Nothing comes easily.'

So how were we supposed to know that in fact the opposite is true if nobody told us? Look around you, the landscape is shifting; neuroscience changed its mind; we are not limited beings as we thought we were 20 years ago. Life does not have to be difficult. *It all depends on what we choose to believe.* We learnt in Quantum Quality Two about **Unlearning** our conditioned behaviour: times change and we must also. Some of what we were taught at school is now obsolete and we have to accept that, let it go, and move on. We all had a unique upbringing, each of us learning a differing 'normal' from our parents, and so of course we had to all turn out differently. Perhaps our parents didn't show us the best way, but we are old enough now to make our own choices and if our behaviour has been abusive to ourselves and/or others then NOW is the time to address this.

The Shift
We will know when this shift occurs as we no longer feel that life is happening *to* us, as pictured on the left, rather we begin to decide for ourselves *how* we are going to live our lives, as depicted on the right. The constant bombardment of outside stimuli just seems to bounce off us, we are better able to cope, and life gets easier.

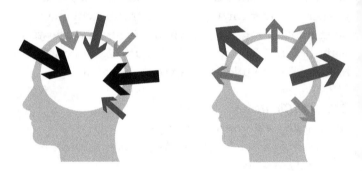

One of the most asked questions from meditation students is,
'Am I doing it right?'

My answer will always be,
'Has your outlook changed? Is life easier?'
If the answer is yes, then you are most definitely doing it right.

Nature Always Shows Us The Way
Picture in your mind a stream. Water always takes the path of least resistance, right? If you place a huge rock right in the middle of the stream it will instantly rearrange itself and move around the rock, continuing its journey as if nothing had happened. Can we take inspiration from

the stream? Can we be as allowing as that? Can we learn to flow *with* life rather than against it?

I knew that I wanted to be surrounded with untouched natural beauty to write this book, as it does indeed inspire me to live my truth. Nature just gets on with it without complaining. There is always flow; the birds don't stop singing just because it's raining; the lettuces don't stop growing because there is a thick fog; and the mountain ponies still take care of their young when the wind is howling through the valley. None of them complain, none of them sulk and feel like a victim, and none of them blames themselves for what is happening in their outer environment.

The Practice As Our Teacher

The present moment is like a mountain: strong, resilient, solid and unfaltering. On it we can watch the clouds passing, allowing them to flow, without wanting to stop them and prevent their journey through the sky. And the clouds keep on coming just like thoughts; which will never *not* exist. We just learn to separate ourselves from their clutch, sitting on our mountain accepting their presence. When we continually come back to the present moment we send a message to the brain, *every single time*, with a new pathway being created. This becomes our new normal. And our minds are so expansive like the sky, we can't possibly know everything or see everything. However, our meditation gives us a flavour of this as we learn to let go of our thoughts and move brain activity to the calmer areas of the brain.

MEDITATION FOUR: Go With The Flow
Hopefully by now you have a set place where you do your daily meditation practice. We are creating a new

habit and you will immediately associate this area of your home with peace, space and connection. Perhaps you could add a candle, incense and a picture of someone who inspires you.

Get settled and close your eyes. Become aware of your breathing, allowing the flow of breath in and out of your body to steady the mind. Step back from your thoughts and begin to watch where the mind wants to go today. Is it into the past? The future? Worrying or planning? Reminiscing perhaps? Detach yourself from it all and let these thoughts pass by without getting involved, knowing that by doing so you are moving brain activity to the quieter more reflective parts of your brain. Do this until you feel relaxed and present.

Then picture yourself in a fast moving stream. You are clinging to the edge and holding on so tight that your fingers are bleeding, terrified of what lies downstream and what will happen to you if you let go. The water is pulling at you but you are adamant that you are staying where you are. What does it feel like to be this scared?

In the end you summon up the courage and go for it, allowing the water to carry you in the path of least resistance. As you float on your back you look up at the sky and scenery as you pass and realise how wonderful it feels to finally flow with life. You accept the journey that the stream is taking you on, effortlessly and naturally navigating the route. Why didn't you do this before?

As you drift you feel all your anxiety release, *left on the waters edge with your fear,* and you enjoy the freedom and liberation of being in flow.

Stay here floating for however long you have, appreciating that decision you finally made to let go…

When it's time to conclude the session bring your hands in a prayer position at your chest and commend yourself for this achievement. The more you do this meditation the more natural it will become to live in the flow of life rather than against it.

Contradicting Myself

There are times, however, that you do need to move *against* the current especially when taking radical action like stopping drinking alcohol or consuming sugar. Because the rest of the world is still doing it, we must in this instance swim *upstream* against the tide of conventional behaviour, but remember we are the advance party and everyone else is going to be following our healthful example sooner or later.

The Opposite Of Addiction ISN'T Sobriety

For too long I tried to be someone that I wasn't; to be popular, liked, prettier, thinner, happier, healthier, fitter. I straddled two worlds for many years as a yoga teacher by day and party animal by night, with my double life nearly driving me crazy for fear of being caught out. I tried to be everything to everyone, a different mask for different sets of friends. Each expecting something from me so I ran around in circles trying to please everyone. Sound familiar?

I felt so disconnected to *myself* that I didn't know what façade to show to the world, and this is what we are now beginning to understand in the world of addiction.

The opposite of addiction isn't sobriety, it's connection

And this information is literally turning everything that we thought we knew about addiction on its head, and this is why...

Rat Heaven
We have all heard of experiments where rats were kept in a cage and given a water bottle with pure water in it and another with water laced with cocaine. The rats preferred the cocaine over the plain water, and the results were clear: cocaine is addictive.

However, Bruce K. Alexander thought to himself that this is not a very realistic experiment and wanted to change a few of the variables to see if the results were the same. He wanted to know why, when we humans are taken very ill and have an operation, we are given a high level dose of pure medical-grade heroin over the course of sometimes weeks or months, but we do not become addicted to it. We are not a society of medical-grade heroin addicts, but why not?

So in 1981 Alexander set out to create Rat Park, which was basically heaven for rats. He built a huge area with different sections for playing and socialising; there were lots of rats of each sex so they could fornicate at will. Plus there was food, water, and also the cocaine-laced water as well. The results were astounding. The rats chose *not* to drink the water spiked with cocaine.

Alexander deduced from this that in the original experiments the rats were drinking the drugs out of boredom and isolation, and if given the option of social interaction and connection to others they would *choose* this over drugs. And this has huge and far-reaching implications. For humans who feel disconnected from society there is a higher potential for addictive tendencies. The flipside of this, of course, is that those who feel understood, supported, listened to and accepted have a far better prognosis to thrive; even more reason to be part of a like-minded community. For if we feel whole then there can be no urge to connect to something that harms us, even if there is a choice for us to do that. The rats chose community, play, and a healthy diet over drugs when given the option and I believe that it is this very concept that plays a huge role in our happiness in sobriety. Get used to saying, feeling, thinking and believing that You Are Enough.

Tip!
Say the words *'I Am Enough'* out loud right now. How do they feel? Do you believe them? In the western world this is a concept that is totally unfamiliar to us, but if you can get into the habit of saying these three words and eventually believing them, they are going to transform your world. Journal how they make you feel today, tomorrow, the next day and on-going until you begin to see a shift in consciousness around how you view yourself. Believe me this technique works; we have used it numerous times within the QS community and the results are life-changing.

Please No More People-Pleasing
Running ragged around everyone else with no regard for yourself has got to stop. It is not serving you and it's time to begin putting yourself first. I still catch myself sometimes people pleasing, and as soon as I do I immediately stop and check in with myself and the Zero Point. *'Be true to yourself Jo, I am enough just as I am'* I will remind myself.

And this is the beauty of the practice; you learn how to be the real you and once you get the hang of it you can get there in an instant. It's not good enough anymore to say nothing to keep the peace, because resentment builds up; that doesn't serve you or the other party. You have to believe that you are enough, and that you deserve to be happy just as much as anyone else in your family/circle/community/job/life.

Do You Feel FULL-filled?

When we are in a state of not feeling enough then obviously that means we think we are lacking something. And when we get that unFULLfilled sensation *within us*, but we mistakenly go looking *externally* to fill the emptiness – **we just gave our power away.**

And this is where compulsive eating, alcohol, shopping, gambling, inappropriate sex and relationships appear to fill that gap and make us feel 'full' for a few minutes, hours or days. Of course this is never going to be satisfying long term because we have placed power in things around us, rather than within, and the answer is to look inward; connect to our own personal power; understand the void and learn to find strength from within. Meditation and reflection are the fast-track to doing this by honouring ourselves and connecting to essence, so that we can find the answers that lie waiting for our readiness to hear and acquire them.

So once we have moved from awareness of lack, taken responsibility by realising that we do have a choice, forgiven ourselves for whatever needed it, then we are in the beautiful sanctified place of acceptance of who we are, *in this very moment*. There isn't anything missing from you, you are whole right now, so it is now totally time to take back your power, thus EMPOWERING yourself.

REFLECTION: **Feeling FULLness**

Wherever you are close your eyes, just for a couple of seconds, and connect to your essence. Notice your breath coming in and out of your body, and notice the sounds and smells of your surroundings. *Now connect to your FULLness. Connect to a feeling of WHOLEness, that you are a complete person with nothing missing.* If this feels strange or unnatural then tell yourself that you are only feeling this for the duration of this short reflection, however, it will become more and more habitual the more you practise it. This FULLness is totally contradictory to compulsive behaviour so the more you can generate the feeling, the less you are going to have the 'urge' to fill yourself up externally.

Journal what you are feeling.

Questions and Answers: **Acceptance**

Q: I simply do not believe that I am enough. In fact the words make me feel horribly uncomfortable. Can I miss this section out?

A: No, this is very significant and central to the process. Say the words out loud at the end of a sitting of meditation, and investigate exactly what is going on. What is driving the belief that you are *not* enough? You are no less deserving of a happy life than anyone else, so getting to the heart of this and moving past it is going to allow a huge breakthrough for you. Stick with it, perhaps journal at length around this subject or speak to a counsellor.

Another tip would be to believe you are enough for only a short time, maybe one day. Get used to the concept and then build up longer times of feeling enough, keep journalling your experience.

Q: In the 'Go With The Flow' meditation I feel out of control and I hate that feeling. How can I stop it?
A: Many of us like to feel in control and it is often this need to control that powers our addiction; our addiction is sometimes the only thing in our lives that we feel we have control over. So letting go of it and going with the flow can be an alien concept yet is one that is going to teach us how to be more flexible in life. Maybe instead visualise yourself at the top of a waterslide and imagine yourself gliding downwards to the awaiting pool. Waterslides are enjoyable and hopefully this will take some of the stress away until you are able to go back to the original visualisation.

Q: I really enjoyed doing the reflection as it's a concept I've not come across before. Could I do this as a meditation?
A: Yes most definitely. The more you get into the vibration of FULLness the less the addictive urge has power; you cannot have both at the same time. So if you would like to spend more time with this new feeling then please do, it is highly beneficial.

Time to move on to our next Quantum Quality.

Quantum Quality Five
Quantum Jumping

*You can have anything because every single possible
potential already exists,
but you can only experience what you believe
and consequently choose*

It's time to start focusing on where we are headed, and
building the future of our dreams. This is where the
magic begins.

I travel to Guatemala regularly to see one of my teachers,
the Chocolate Shaman, and he likes to give a teaching
about life as buses.

- **The hard bus**: the one we have all been on for
  the whole of our lives and where all addiction
  travels;
- **The easy bus**: which we are now starting to
  experience on the Quantum Sobriety journey;
- **The magic bus**: a route that we've not been on
  before and seems so idealistic that we believe it to
  be totally impossible.

We are no different from anyone else; we deserve a
dream life just as much as this or that other person who
seems to 'have it all'. Each human body contains the same
organs, lives on the same earth and breathes in the same
air. Yes we are born into different circumstances but some
use adversity to become stronger and teach others how to

do the same, whilst others use hardship as an excuse to play victim their whole lives.

For most of us we have been walking this earth with a blindfold on, not realising that we are in fact allowed to be happy and are deserving of an abundant life. But how were we supposed to know this with our media bombarding us with images of difficulty and lack?

Mind Your Language
We must start to watch our words to our beautiful self. Do we naturally put ourselves down and talk ourselves out of what we really want? The challenge is to STOP negative self-defeating language completely. So the following is now totally banned from your vocabulary:

- I can't
- I'm not clever enough
- I'm not pretty enough
- I'm not thin enough
- I have no money
- Life is so hard
- It's not fair
- I hate my life

You get my drift! These statements are pretty obvious and will be the first set of beliefs that will be eliminated from your mind, easily I hope. For as soon as you utter these words the quantum gives you people, situations and experiences to MATCH what you have uttered:

'I'm not clever enough' you say.
'OK' replies your quantum friend, *'I won't give you that promotion that you were just about to receive.'*

Or how about:

'It's not fair' you say.

'Oh, is that what you think?' replies the quantum, *'Then I will give you something really juicy and awful to MATCH that belief.'*

Your servant is always listening. Even when you don't say it out loud, just in your head, so it is imperative that you start to notice what you believe, and therefore are saying. And most of the time we have the same stuff looping around our minds over and over again.

'We are what we think. All that we are arises with our thoughts. With our thoughts we make the world'
Buddha

Next Step
Once we have eradicated the toxic self-chat we uncover the next layer of dialogue that we are having with ourselves.

The following examples are where most people who begin on this path stumble. They sound better than the above statements but are still not quite right:

- I hope I can stay sober
- I want to be rich
- I am going to be a healthy weight
- I wish I could be happy
- I will be healthy when…

We are still not fully taking responsibility here and are pushing where we would **prefer** to be off out there in the future, it's not in our sphere of NOW, and therefore will remain out of reach for us.

This is now what the quantum is hearing:

'I hope I can stay sober,' you say
'You only hope? You don't believe it?' answers the quantum field, *'Then nor do I, here is a situation where you are going to be hugely triggered.'*

Or this:
'I want to be rich,' you say
'So you don't really believe that you can be then?' is the response, *'Then I will give you the same financial situations as you've always had.'*

And so nothing changes, we go around and around in circles like this, believing that we really, really 'want' and 'wish' that our lives could be better but *still* inadvertently push away that which we truly desire.

I **AM**

It is time to learn a new language just like you did at school or since; it's going to be exactly the same. Now you begin your sentences with 'I am...'

You move your language *out* into the future, marrying it and your dreams in the present.

- I am sober
- I am rich
- I am a healthy weight
- I am happy

Now you are having the following conversation with the quantum realm:

'I am rich,' you say
'OK, I hear you,' the quantum replies, 'Here is some money.'

Or:
'I am a healthy weight,'
'OK, I hear you' responds the quantum, 'Look at these delicious new healthy cakes/crackers/snacks that you've never seen before.'

Been To The Optician Lately?
Suddenly you see differently, you notice other objects/events/items that you've never seen before. And just like when you are tested for a new prescription and the optician places different lenses in the makeshift glasses, with each new lens comes a different sight; a new potential. You choose, and no one else can choose for you. We each have our own mind-optician busy at all times of the day getting our personal unique prescription ready, and she is listening to *all* of our needs. She is hot on customer service and her objective is to meet every single one of your requests as quickly as she can:

'I am so fat,' you say
'No problem madam,' she replies, 'Here is some more fat for you. Would you like an extra two or four pounds today?'

Be careful of your language and begin to consciously create what you actually want, rather than unconsciously manifesting the complete opposite.

Vision Boarding

I have been using vision boards for over 10 years with great success. My first 'evidence' occurred when I put up a picture of my sister and brother-in-law (picture on the left) who have a loving relationship; one that I aspired to having myself. A few years later when attending a friend's wedding with my new boyfriend (who later became my husband) a photographer was snapping away and I didn't pay much attention to him. A few weeks later my friend sent me through some photos of the wedding and to my great surprise there was a picture of Dom and me (picture on the right) that was set up in EXACTLY the same way as the one of my sister and brother-in-law. It was uncanny and almost a little scary! *And in both photos all parties had no idea the picture had been taken.* This was my first taste of conscious manifestation and to say that it whet my appetite is an understatement. It was evidence that vision boards work, and I then felt a boundless excitement about what I was going to put on my board next!

A 'Trick' Of The Mind

This manifestation lark gets easier with practice, and means when you first start out on this path you almost have to 'trick' your mind into believing that it's possible. With time this new muscle becomes strong and flexible and we manifest with ease.

'It's not working.'
'It doesn't work for me.'
'I'm really trying but I just can't change.'

These are protests that I hear all of the time, and really it's understandable because we are doing something quite radical here. We are going against all that we've ever been taught before, by refusing to accept to play small any longer. But trust me it does get easier once you gain confidence in the method and start to see your own evidence. Begin with some simple ideas that will get the ball rolling, and then watch your tiny golf ball snowball into the most amazing manifestations of your wildest dreams.

EXERCISE ELEVEN: **The Vision Board**

Now it's time to make a vision board. Maybe you have one already, or perhaps you've not made one before. Either way it's good to make new ones, at least once per year. You are going to need:

- Large A3 (or bigger) piece of thick paper/card
- Old magazines
- Scissors
- Glue
- One hour of your time

Do you remember the questions I asked you right at the beginning of the Quantum Qualities? And the Bagua? These are going to come into play now. The Bagua template contains nine boxes which signify the main areas of your life, and you are going to divide up your plain piece of paper so that you have these nine areas marked (you can actually do that or just know where each section is).

Then have a think about each area. What is your dream for each? If you could have anything in each area what would it be? What does your dream job look like?

Wealth	Reputation	Love
Health	Wellbeing	Family
Knowledge	Career	Spirituality

What does your dream relationship look like? What is your ideal earning potential? How could you be healthier? What makes you happy?

The idea is that you really 'think outside the box'. This book is all about taking limitations off and thinking big.

Many, many people I have taught have struggled to get off the starting line with their vision boards, with comments like:

'I have no idea what I want, Jo.'

'I already have everything in my life that I could ever need.'

'I don't deserve my dreams.'

Don't worry I've heard it all before! And it took me time, too, to get in the swing of things. We have probably never been told before that we can have *anything*. Our lives have been shrouded in lack, limitation and struggle; what I call 'poverty consciousness'. And the vision board is the best way to get you out.

So, once you've had a think about each area you need to find images and words that capture your dream perfectly, and remember the rules...

- Always use language in the present tense
- Think big
- You can only do this for yourself; not for others' wellbeing/happiness

Begin by looking through magazines for images that resonate, or perhaps you would like to use a picture of you with your partner/spouse in happier times; an era that you would like to recreate. Sometimes when we are looking through magazines we get inspired if we don't really know what exactly we are looking for, but don't get distracted and start reading articles. There is work to be done and a fabulous future to create!

If you can't find the right images or you know exactly what you are looking for you can also search for images on the internet and then print them off. I drag these images into a word document and resize them and then print out the whole page so that they fit nicely on my vision board.

You don't have to just use images, you can also use text cut out from magazines or written directly onto the page. Just remember to keep the words in the present tense.

Time To Believe In Magic
Place your completed vision board on the wall where you will see it every day yet not somewhere that people visiting you will see, ideally in your bedroom or office. I had one client who was so busy with work and his young family that he had it on the inside of his toilet door, as this was the only place in his house where he could be alone! He did also have a copy of it in his work locker.

The idea is that you look at your vision board everyday. These visions are seeds that you have planted and every time you look at and think about them you are watering your dreams.

'I don't think it's working,' you say.
'Don't you?' replies the quantum, *'OK, I agree, no, it isn't.'*
or
'I am sober and I can't believe how easy it is,' you say.
'That's great,' responds your friend, *'Here's some more ease in other areas of your life too then.'*

Then it's time to **believe**. The magic isn't going to work if you don't.

Know that the job that you dream of is just about to be offered to you. Believe it into reality.

Know that love is just around the corner; your dream partner is getting ready for you while you are getting yourself ready for them; it's about to happen magically. Think about it this way: your soulmate is looking for you too, they are *waiting* for you to get into the right frame of mind (at the moment you are energetically *pushing them away* otherwise they would be here already).

Know that you deserve sobriety and the freedom that comes with it. Know that you have taken your last drink/ cigarette/sugar-laden cake/online gamble/line of coke/ inappropriate sexual encounter, and you couldn't be happier about it. Just because it seems that everyone else is doing it doesn't mean you are going to continue to live a mediocre life.

Know that you no longer need to emotionally eat, numb out from life through booze or create a screen of smoke between you and the world. Through meditation you are getting to know yourself and dealing with your demons, so now there is no need to pretend to be someone else or hide behind a substance.

Quantum Manifestation

OK, are you ready? This is where things start to really heat up.

We know that when the mind goes somewhere there is always going to be a chemical response; so by taking ourselves to something that is on our vision board, our body *has to* react.

We are actually creating the feeling of the *outcome* in our body; which doesn't know the difference between what is happening now, in the past, or the future.

The body always listens to the brain. So as we begin to visualise the wonderful loving relationship that we are about to manifest, the frontal lobe activates, and because this area of the brain is connected to all other parts it sends out a message looking for similar relationships/ events that have happened in the past. Just like a computer search, all relevant neural networks (computer files) are found and produced to the boss (frontal lobe). The brain is reorganising itself and creating something new from the information that we've just given it (vision board pictures) and memories of something similar that's happened in our past. As soon as this occurs there is of course a chemical reaction in the body, hormones, etc, and we feel different. If we are doing this over and over again we can teach the body and brain what it feels like to have this amazing relationship, to the extent that the body and brain think it is already real.

We have now expanded ourselves to be in the present but living in the future, rather than being bound to the past.

This is how we manifest on the quantum level, and although it may feel like we are 'tricking' ourselves at first, once we understand and begin to see that it works it becomes second nature to do this all of the time. We begin to live our lives out there in the pure potentiality of the future and quantum realms.

MEDITATION FIVE: An Alternate Reality
Sit in your favourite place to meditate and get comfortable. Make sure nothing is going to distract you; your phone is off, the door is closed so that the cat/dog can't get in, and your family are instructed not to disturb you. Set the timer to however long you are committing to

this meditation.

Place your hands in your lap or on your knees and close your eyes. Become aware of your breathing and of how you feel in this moment: are you warm? Cool? Stressed? Calm? Are you excited to do the next meditation and create a different reality for yourself?

Begin to familiarise yourself with 'the gap', watching your thoughts from a distant place rather than getting caught up in them. Come back to your breathing over and over again. Stay here 'stabilising' for a few minutes, or more if you have longer.

Now walk over to an archway. On the other side of this archway is an alternate reality where all of the dreams you have placed on your vision board are already realised; they're happening.

Stand in the archway and notice from this vantage point all of the different areas of your life. Maybe stick an arm through and see if you can feel the changes. Stay here for a while observing.

Then step through to this alternate reality. What does it look, feel, smell, sound and taste like here?

After a few minutes notice one particular event that is on your vision board, in just one of the areas of your life, and begin to see this dream as if it were already happening. You're trying it on for size: what does it look, feel, smell, sound and taste like? Use your senses as much as you can to create the feeling in both your brain and subsequently your body. Revel in the feeling for a few minutes; allowing the image to become so real that you believe it is happening. Stay here for as long as you have in this session.

Then let the visualisation go and come back to your breathing again.

Now come back to your old reality and notice the difference. Where would you rather be? And if it is in the alternate reality then make that choice and step back through the archway for good, this is your new home now, you know that you do in fact deserve to live in this heightened parallel universe. *You just quantum jumped.*

When you are ready or when your timer sounds start to move your fingers and toes and stretch your body. Bring your hands in a prayer position in front of your heart and thank yourself for believing.

Shifting Into Different Realities

Everything is possible, and everything that has ever happened has done so inside the field of your consciousness. There is no reality or experience outside of consciousness, objects do not have beingness themselves, they need consciousness to exist. So *you* hold all of the power, *you* are the centre of your universe, everything is spinning around and dependent on *you*.

Lets take the example of dreaming. We know that it is part of us yet it doesn't seem real, but dreams can't exist on their own without consciousness; they are happening in another reality though, this is clear. So already we can grasp the concept of alternate realities, yes?

And if consciousness energy has been involved with every single experience that we've ever had, it would be fair to say that it can shape itself into anything. This means that wherever we shift our consciousness to will determine our experience. Please fully take this on board;

the power that we have over our lives if we fully harness this amazing quantum energy.

Now think about a movie and all of the frames that it is made up of. Slow the reel down and look at two frames that are side by side; when you look at each image on its own, each one is complete. And from the perspective of the image it has no concept of the other because it is whole and its molecules have no relationship to its neighbours. These two frames are parallel realities and demonstrate the potential that we can also welcome into our own lives.

Everything Exists
Let's go even further; every single potential experience has already been formed, so we don't actually create new events; we simply *choose* which wave form we want to collapse in any given situation from an unlimited selection. Everything that could have ever happened in our past existed (and still does) and everything that's possible for our future already exists (and always will). Each potential is like a frame in a movie; each nanosecond of our lives a frame and we jump from frame to frame, or reality to reality. There is always choice and the more you understand this the more conscious of your creations you become, and life becomes easier and more enjoyable because at last you know the rules.

You can have anything because every single possible potential already exists, but you can only experience what you believe and consequently choose.

The Seven Circles Of Possibility
Let's investigate this theory in relation to addiction. Each different coloured circle represents a potential reality:

Red: addicted and not even aware of the fact
Orange: addicted and aware but not ready to change (denial)
Yellow: addicted and beginning to look for a solution
Green: addicted and following a course of action
Blue: sober but struggling and finding it difficult
Indigo: Quantum Sobriety, or *freedom* in sobriety
Purple: beyond addiction

RED   ORANGE YELLOW GREEN   BLUE   INDIGO   PURPLE

We all know someone in each of these realities and have probably experienced many of them (if not all) at one time or another ourselves, so we can understand that *all of them* are possible. This means that Quantum Sobriety (and beyond) is available to you, and all you have to do is choose that reality.

But how?

The answer is so simple yet takes a monumental leap of faith: all you have to do is believe it. Believe *freedom* in your sobriety into reality; live in that reality rather than the one of struggle. Once your mind-set shifts to this new location it is so easy to comprehend and you wonder why you never jumped into this parallel universe before.

You are choosing your reality every single second with all options available at every turn. At a quantum level think of each coloured circle as electrons which are at this point just a wave of probability, remembering that there has to be an observer (us) to make anything happen. So these circles are all vying for our attention,

'Pick me,' says blue.
'No me' shouts orange. *'You chose blue yesterday.'*
'I think you'll all find it's my turn,' cries green.

And then you and only you decide in that moment which wave function you are going to collapse and, therefore, which experience you have chosen to have.

REFLECTION: **Quantum Jumping**

Close your eyes and become aware of your breathing and of your surroundings; are you warm? Are you tired? Are you hungry?

Then think about the person that you want to be, and take yourself to that future self. What are you *now* feeling? What does this future you look like? How does this future you speak? Really get into the role of being this other person. Maybe in the beginning it feels like you are acting and this other person is not you, but the more you do this the more you *become* the future you. *Act like you are the you that you want to be, and you will be the person that you prefer to be.*

Journal your experience each time you quantum jump like this.

Questions and Answers: **Quantum Jumping**

Q: I find it very difficult to pretend that everything is going to be ok when I don't think it is.

A: In the beginning it is a challenge to get yourself into the future and out of the past, but trust me it does get easier. It is a muscle that you've not used before, and when we start any new sport there is an initial stage of trying. Just think of learning to swim or ski. Much like meditation too, in the beginning it's the most difficult but it will always improve with practice, that's why the word PRACTICE means just that: practice to make perfect.

If you 'don't think' anything is going to change, then it won't; that is what you have chosen. Somehow, even if it is just for the meditation in the beginning, you start by 'pretending' and then it gets much easier to do.

Q: This concept of quantum jumping seems very far-fetched and extremely unrealistic! I'm having a hard time understanding it.

A: I will agree that it goes against everything that we've perhaps been taught thus far in life and this is because it's new information. Quantum physics is a very recent discovery in the grand scheme of things and it is only relatively recently that we have learnt that our minds are not fixed. So ease yourself slowly into this new arena; keep meditating everyday with the meditations given in this book so that you can unlearn negative neural networks and create new more expansive ones. There is no need to rush.

Time to move on to our next Quantum Quality.

Quantum Quality Six
Perspective

We quite literally cannot NOT learn this method;
our lives depend on it for sure

It's at this point that I am going to ask you to start thinking in an opposite way to how you have been doing so in life thus far. We have got so much back to front, and then wonder why we're poor emotionally, spiritually, physically as well as financially. We are always trying to 'fit' our meditation around our lives, whereas the truth is *our lives depend on it*. Why then do we continue to keep that which feeds our soul at such a low priority in our day?

I have answers here in this book, but you have to come with me on this one and start to take a look at your life from the outside, with some **perspective**. If we can only see what we believe to be true, then to experience change in our lives we must shift our perception of things; we cannot stay the same.

Think about your beliefs around what is possible for you financially. Where are you right now? Broke? Just about getting by? Comfortable? Affluent? You can only experience what you believe so your current external money situation *has* to be a reflection of what's going on internally. So whatever your set of beliefs is around money that you are holding in your mind right now, there

is at this time no extra room for additional money.
For any change to happen we must first EXPAND our
mind-set to make room for this to occur. Imagine your
mind expanding and all of that new extra EMPTY space
just waiting for the money (love, happiness, good health:
fill in what you want more of) to fall into.

BUT without the expansion nothing more is going to
fit in, so it has to happen *first*. This is a huge factor and
because of this order of things people very often just
can't get their heads around the inner expansion *before*
they've seen the outer manifestation and, therefore, this is
where they falter.

Right at the beginning in our very first Quantum Quality
and meditation we found space and touched in on our
essence. Quality Six is going deeper so that we make time
in our lives regularly to gain perspective constantly .

The Big Rocks
So how do we put our lives back together, now that we've
taken them apart, in a more constructive way? Well we
prioritise.

Big rocks = meditation and self-care
Pebbles = family and work
Sand = day to day phone calls, housework, emails and
washing

If you fill a jar with sand first and add pebbles on top,
then you will not have any space remaining for the
big rocks. However, if you place the big rocks in first
(meditation and self-care), then the pebbles which will
fall around the big rocks (family, work, etc.), then the
sand is easily going to fit too, as it splashes effortlessly
around everything else (day-to-day phone calls,

housework, meetings, emails, washing). So you can see the problem that most of us face; our biggest rock should be meditation rather than it being the smallest (probably) up until now, so we need to make time for it and factor it into our day.

Brain Waves
Our amazing brain is capable of a number of different 'speeds' which help us function in all manner of situations. We must slow down to sleep and meditate, yet need alertness and pace when we're working, exercising or holding a conversation. To read brain waves we use an EEG (electroencephalograph) machine which when worn looks like you're wearing a cap of wires. This equipment reads the electromagnetic charges that are released when neurons are firing, so every thought and emotion is recorded.

- **Delta** waves: these are very slow and this is when we are in a deep sleep
- **Theta** waves: these are slightly quicker and are when we are waking up, in a lucid state, or in deep meditation.
- **Alpha** waves: these are needed for imagination and creativity, looking inward we feel more connected to ourselves, we are in a light meditative state
- **Beta** waves: our regular waking state of conscious thought and outer stimulation, reading, writing, thinking and processing.
- **Gamma** waves: these are seen in elevated states of consciousness.

When Is The Best Time To Meditate?
Our journey into meditation goes from Beta to Alpha to Theta, and what I have found over the years is that to

practice first thing in the morning when my brain is still waking up is the absolute best time.

Before I researched all of this I used to do the opposite; I did rigorous exercise first, drank loads of caffeine thinking that I was going to be more 'alert' and then expected my brain to calm down! Now that I understand *how* the brain is working I do the reverse; on waking I immediately go and sit on my cushion and make the most of my slow brain waves. I can get into a relaxed state of mind so much easier *because it is already there*. This has revolutionised my daily routine and level of meditation = more connection and more happiness.

What Time Of Day Should You Meditate?
This is the million-dollar question. Up until a number of years ago I was a lifelong lover of lay-ins and found morning meditation a real challenge. If I didn't meditate in the morning (a big rock) then quite often I found that I'd gone the whole day without doing it at all, as getting pulled off in this direction and that is all too easy. It's like the day draws you away and you've missed the bus altogether. Sometimes I would then get on my cushion in the afternoon but nine times out of ten it just didn't happen. So I started to do something radical. Something that I had not done ever before in my life...

I began to get up earlier than I needed to so that I could meditate without rushing.

This was such a big deal for me, and an absolute game changer. I haven't looked back and now it is EASY to get up earlier, it is just a case of rewiring that belief you hold about yourself. I turned, *'I'm not a morning person,'* which I believed for more than 40 years, into, *'I get up by 6am everyday no matter what, to meditate.'*

And I love it. I have em**POWER**ed myself in an instant. And the strange thing is that I now jump out of bed *with enthusiasm* (although admittedly that didn't happen straight away, there was a period of adjustment), and I can honestly say that it was shocking to me, and those who know me well. Whoever regretted getting up early to do something worthwhile? And how many times have you regretted *not* getting up and missing out on a great sunrise, or doing your practice?

If you have a family then getting up before everyone else may be the quietest time of the day for you, and this is going to become your favourite time of day I promise.

All ultra successful people have a morning routine, so that they can get ahead of the game before the rest of the world wakes up. You do have to look at your evening routine too though, as I discovered when I first began to get up earlier; it ended in complete burnout because I was still going to bed at the same time! So now I go to bed earlier too, and the really great thing about this is that I have begun to wake up a couple of minutes before my alarm; how fabulous is that?

Tip!
Get up at the same time, *even on your day off,* so that your body can get used to that hour. Laying in on your day off puts your body clock out so that it will never get used to a particular hour. This was a huge shift for me when I began to get up by 6am also on my day off; the day seemed to go on forever, it was wonderful.
Plus it seemed like I felt that I 'deserved' a lay-in but what it actually did was make me feel like I was trying to catch up all day, which was horrible. So now my mind-set has

shifted totally to feeling that I 'deserve' to wake up early and make the most of my life, every day.

Evening Is OK Too
First thing in the morning may not be the right time for your practice, however, and the priority here is to create a new habit that is sustainable. It's more important that you are meditating everyday than what time that happens to be.

If your job gets you up at the crack of dawn then it's a big ask to get up even earlier so an evening routine may suit you better. Another great time is when you first get in from work, to transition from the workday to evening, but even better than that is the hour before bed, for this should ensure a delightful night's rest.

Putting down computers and phones a few hours before bed is highly recommended, and creating a wonderfully relaxing evening routine is going to support a great night's sleep so that you wake up full of beans and beginning the next day in the best possible way. Here are some ideas:
- Meditate
- Hot bath
- Read a book
- Make a list of what you are doing tomorrow so that you are not thinking about work through the night
- Journal: this can have the same effect as the work list: by getting out on paper what has happened during the day you don't carry it into your sleep/ dreams
- Gratitude diary (see next chapter for details)
- Lavender essential oil on your pillow

Why Are You Rushing?

The next factor to start thinking about is slowing down and being more organised. Going back to our brain waves, there are three levels of Beta (our conscious day-to-day state) and we need to be mindful of which one we are operating from.

1. **Low**: Relaxed yet aware. You are fully engaged with your outer environment, enjoying a walk around your garden and taking in the smells, sights and sounds.
2. **Mid**: More alert now. There is something going on in the next garden to ours, and we are wondering what.
3. **High**: Your neighbour comes out of their house and starts to shout and becomes threatening. Your brain immediately becomes over-stimulated and you can feel the release of stress chemicals into your body as you enter the fight or flight state.

For many of us we are living from this third state most of the time, and it is having a hugely detrimental effect on our wellbeing. This is not where we want our 'normal' set-point to be as this will encourage illness, dis-ease, unhappiness and keep us bound to the cycle of addiction. There is no freedom in high Beta. We are going to start noticing it in our bodies when we switch to an unhealthy amount of stress. This state is cumulative too, so left unchecked it will rise and rise becoming what we believe is normal, until we quite literally 'explode' with high blood pressure, anxiety, indigestion, depression or worse.

Every day we must check in with ourselves and make sure we are not operating from high Beta but instead in the lower ranges. And we can create certain procedures to ensure this is happening:

1. Prioritising: meditation and self-care must come first.
2. Planning: making sure you are not cramming too much into your day, as this is a sure fire way of instantly creating stress.
3. Nutrition: you need the right foods to keep you on track (more about nutrition in the Helpers section, see p.233).
4. Asking for help: this can be difficult for a lot of us as we soldier on trying to cope as best we can, putting a brave face on it, but underneath the *'Yes, everything is fine'* pretence we are screaming for support.
5. Leave enough time: rushing around like a headless chicken is putting stress on your system. I did this relatively recently but caught myself just before I drove myself mad.

If we ensure the above then moving from high Beta to the mid or low point is going to become easy to establish and maintain.

The Girl Who Missed Her Train
I was going into town one morning, woke up late, didn't have time for meditation (this was before I started to get up earlier for meditation), and rushed, rushed, rushed. I drove to the station and just as I pulled into the car park my train pulled out of the platform. Now I live in the sticks and there is only one train *per hour* so I was pretty much screwed. I decided I was going to have to drive to another station, which was 40 minutes away but had more frequent trains, and found myself in the car shouting at no one in particular,
'Quick, come on, I'm going to be sooooo late.'
Once at the second station I got on the next train into London and swiftly arrived at Stratford. Here I raced off,

down the steps, along the tunnel, ran up the steps, saw my next train in its platform, jumped on it, raced all the way along it as I knew that the exit at my destination was at the other end of the train. As I was pacing through the carriages I noticed a lady sitting down who was reading the very same Buddhist book that I was currently reading, and as soon as the title registered in my brain it was like all the wind had been taken out of my sails.

The quantum just threw me a huge message

And I understood it, suddenly seeing my behaviour of the last few hours from a different perspective; how I had jumped on the high Beta horse and galloped at the highest speed across the fields with no thought and no reason. I hadn't got to London any quicker than if I had calmed myself down and spent the hour on the train meditating, changing the chemicals my brain was sending my body and all in all having a much nicer journey.

I sat down immediately and took stock of the situation, noticing the addictive sequence of events I had set off from a solitary incident and wondering if I would have continued like that all day had I not had my eyes open to the message that came in from source. I know that had I continued like that I would have bumped up against other high Beta bunnies all being attracted to the same high stress situations, and driving each other mad. There would have been huffing and puffing, pushing, dirty looks and impatience; and ALL of this because I missed a train.

When you can break stress down into sizeable pieces like this, and see where your weak points are then it's so much easier to remedy your environment. Now, I would be up early doing my meditation, creating enough time to get ready and out of the door with plenty of time to spare to pay for parking and wait for the train. It can be so simple if we choose to make it so.

EXERCISE TWELVE: Silence

Have you ever spent a period of time in silence? Do you think you could do it? This brings up an awful lot of resistance in people but I think they may be missing the point. What silence does, especially being around people who are talking, is show us how much of what we usually say is meaningless. Do we really need to be nattering away to everyone all day long? What are we really scared of by quietening our minds down?

Silence is a brilliant way of giving us an additional dimension of perspective; what do we want to say? And do we really need to say it?

What you will find *after* a set period of silence is that you will speak less, you become automatically more mindful of what you say, and words become vehicles of your soul rather than random ramblings.

Set aside a few hours once a week or month to be silent. Tell your family what you are doing, and even though they may think you are a bit bonkers at the beginning of this journey, ultimately they are going to notice your elevated energy, attitude and devotion to them and will begin to get to know and love this new 'enhanced' you. Perhaps you can commit to a whole 24-hour period of silence and see what a transformation it can make to your perception of life. However long you choose to be silent for, when you speak again your words will feel exquisite and become more precious; you will not want to waste them again.

Tolerance

Our next meditation is going to be a sound meditation. No matter where you meditate there is always sound – when I was teaching in Thailand the sound of jungle life was sometimes deafening. Again it comes down to our mind-set (I hope you are seeing that EVERYTHING in life comes down to it) and in the sound meditation we are going to accept all of the sounds that we hear in the allotted time, whether we *like* them or not. We cannot stop the plane from crossing the sky, the seagull from squawking or the conversation happening outside our window. Instead we connect to the space that is in between us and the sound, in the same way we connect to the space between us and our thoughts. Let's give it a go…

MEDITATION SIX: The Sound Meditation

You may like to use an app of singing bowls sounding at intervals, which is a technique that I use in my classes. Bowls are sometimes used as an aid in group sound meditations, and there are a few apps now where you can program different bowls to chime at certain intervals. This may or may not be helpful to you.

Get comfortable on your cushion and set your timer for however long you have to meditate. Keep your back straight and close your eyes.

Notice sounds that are far away in the distance, outside your home. Then bring your attention into the house and the sounds that your family or housemates are making. Does the heating make a sound? Perhaps there is rain splashing on the windows or wind howling about the place? Then come into the room, what sounds are there here? Is there a clock? A radiator clicking? Perhaps you

can hear your breath or your tummy rumbling?
The point here is to notice but not to listen for sounds, there is a subtle difference. Just as we have been using the breath up until now to rest our minds upon, we are going to use the sounds around us. And it doesn't matter about how noisy our home is; in fact the sounds are helping us by reminding us to come back to the present moment over and over again. Each sound becomes an opportunity to be nudged out of thought and back to the present moment.

We stay present, dropping into the silence, then a thought comes in and takes us away, then we hear something, we become present again, we let go of our thoughts. Over and over again.
In the end we realise that the noises are not distracting and annoying us any longer, they are in fact *helping*. When we realise this we understand the sound meditation, and it becomes like a friend. We then *welcome* sounds, each one keeping us on track, here, now, where the magic is.
Continue like this until your timer rings.

Overview
This meditation is excellent for changing our perspective on sound in meditation: becoming tolerant of it. What we are learning about ourselves during our practice we naturally take over into all areas of our lives and, therefore, we learn the art of tolerance in everyday life.

Conclusion
Just like a fish out of water battles to stay alive, we too spend our lives struggling when we live from a high Beta state. A fish will ultimately die when left out of water and we too will catch a stress born illness if we remain in a

reactive place. Yet as soon as we drop down into the deep waters of our minds we find respite, peace and space, so why on earth are we not living from this place? We quite literally cannot NOT learn this method; our lives depend on it for sure.

Your practice will change and mature; the more effort you put in the more peace you will experience, it is a simple exchange. And you will learn and experience the different states; when you slip into a low Beta stage in meditation or when you have sunk into Alpha or even the elusive Theta state.

You will begin to get to know your mind and the games it likes to play, egging you on to ever more pressure, status or responsibility (the ego). You have to work out what is important in your life; do you want to be free? And if so then meditation is the fast-track way of getting there. Yes you can do it other ways but nothing is going to get you to this destination in a more direct route.

Tip!

On retreat with Lama Yeshe Rinpoche, the Abbott of Samye Ling monastery in Scotland a few years ago he told the story of when he went into a long silent retreat in the USA. Literally as soon as the retreat started building work began within the monastery, right next to where he was staying. During the day it was very noisy and his mind protested, *'I cannot meditate!'* and, *'How am I supposed to meditate with this noise!'*, and he fought and fought with himself within his own mind.

Months passed and the new structure took shape and by the time it was finished Lama had realised that it had taken place right next to him to teach him to practise no matter what was going on around him. Now he is able to meditate anywhere because of this excellent training that he was given!

REFLECTION: **Perspective**
Perhaps you have noticed that your perception has changed already, since beginning this book? Maybe you are seeing your world in a slightly altered state, and can see from a different perspective? This is the wonderful aspect of journalling as it chronicles our life adventure, and if you resonate with this approach and follow the exercises and meditations you ARE going to shift your perceptions.

Questions and Answers: **Perspective**

Q: I am most definitely not a morning person and I will struggle to get up before I have to. Do you have any more advice or tips for creating this new routine?

A: Like any of these new techniques and beliefs there is going to be a period of adjustment. But once you have made the decision to rewire your brain in that way then it is just a matter of time before the new behaviour becomes your new normal. Take driving on the opposite side of the road when you visit another country; in the beginning you keep reaching for the gears on the wrong side and second guess yourself when going around a roundabout, but after a day or two it becomes second nature: neurons are firing and creating a new pathway so your brain is changing to accommodate your new habit.

And believe me I do sympathise as I was exactly like you a few years ago. But once I'd made the decision that my meditation practice was vital to my mental health, then I created a new reality and it became easy. Try it and you may also be surprised.

Q: I'm scared that I am going to change so much that my family are not going to be able to connect to who I am changing into.

A: Please do not worry about that, for you are morphing into *more* of who you really are.

You are becoming the highest version of you possible, and they will love you all the more for it.

Time to move on to our next Quantum Quality.

Quantum Quality Seven
Gratitude

Gratitude opens the door for generosity, for when we feel abundant it is easier to give to others that which we already have

Gratitude is one of life's currencies, and when you give it out to others the quantum immediately creates more situations to feel grateful for. It is one of our building blocks to the amazing future that we are carving out for ourselves, opening us up to so much more.

Tibetan Buddhism believes we have been given a *'precious human life'*, in which we have the opportunity to do so much. So just being alive, in a body, gives rise for gratitude. Then to be in a position to be reading this book and having the insight to become the best person we possibly can, we really do have such a lot to be thankful for.

Developing Gratitude

I have written this book whilst on retreat myself – I always try to do two personal retreats per year, with my own Buddhist practice being Chenrezig. Once a year I complete between four and eight 'pairs' of Nyungneys; the fasting ritual of the Buddhist deity of compassion. It is beautiful and something that I am very committed to doing annually.

During this retreat there is an opportunity for lay people

to take monastic vows, and these are taken each morning at the beginning of the first (of three) daily sessions. The practice is performed over two days and you can choose how many 'pairs' you want to do; on the first day of each pair there is one meal at lunchtime and drinks served at allocated times (you are not allowed to get your own food and drink on this retreat, it has to be given to you at the assigned breaks). On the second day of each pair there is no food, no drinks and silence.

It is hard, and it is meant to be. There are many reasons behind this, some of which are:

- To become more mindful of what you say, eat and drink
- To concentrate and devote oneself to the practice and meditation
- To develop compassion. Through fasting we experience discomfort of the body and mind, and feel kinship with those that do not have food and water available in their day-to-day existence.
- We learn how to deal with our feelings. Normally if we feel hungry we reach for something to eat; if we have something to say we say it; and if we are thirsty we take a drink. *We immediately stop the uncomfortable feeling.* When we take vows not to do these things we can begin to explore the sensations and associated emotions therein.

What Are You Feeling?

This goes so deep. As soon as we feel something unpleasant we stuff it down with food, alcohol or drugs. We have a headache and immediately take a pill, rather than looking at why we have a headache, for the body is communicating with us but we ignore the message and carry on with our busy lives. In retreat we get to question what is going on so that we can understand ourselves better, and because we have taken a vow and committed to omit distractions it is like giving *yourself* a gift.

When we desire something be it food, water (during the practice) or alcohol, binge-eating, or angry words, we immediately satisfy ourselves and fulfil the craving, thus running away from our feelings and a potential insight/learning.

The Buddha says it is like drinking salty water: the more we drink the thirstier we become, thus perpetuating the cycle over and over again. And isn't this exactly what we are doing with our addictions to food, alcohol and drugs? Putting plaster after plaster over the wound, and simply not being willing to deal with what is festering underneath.

Fasting Day

I cannot explain the absolute and unconditional gratitude that I feel after a period of fasting. The first drink after 36 hours of drought is magical; like your body waking up from the semi-coma it has to reach to survive (there is much pain in the body from meditating for around eight hours a day as well as the weakness from lack of nutrients and water); the first food after 48 hours tastes like sweet nectar and the most divine thing you've ever consumed. However, for me speaking comes back very slowly. From a place of stillness and silence it's like that ability has to be woken up slowly, and with respect. I find this the easiest aspect of our abstention.

On our residential Quantum Sobriety retreat we have a day of fasting (we do still have liquids), and part of the day in silence to demonstrate how we can experience sensations of craving without immediately covering them over, and to generate feelings of humility, compassion and gratitude. For some who have never spent a day without food and don't think they will survive, it's wonderful to watch how empowered they become at the end of the day when they realise how strong their minds really are, and experience an overwhelming taste of gratitude. Plus they can also transfer the success of doing something that they thought they couldn't to their budding sobriety.

Choosing To Fast
I know that the retreat that I do yearly is hard-core and I'm not suggesting for a second that you should do similar but perhaps taking half a day per week (or a full day if you feel confident) to fast (no food, but still have liquids) and have an extended meditation session, will take your practice through the roof. If you can dedicate this time to yourself you will experience all of the Quantum Qualities and when you taste your first food in the afternoon/evening you will feel gratitude like never before. For me *choosing* to fast is so beautiful when there are so many on our planet who are starving, and when I am fasting I think of them and send love.

Sometimes the first taste of food/drink after fasting is so powerfully humbling that there are many tears. Tears for those who do not have what is rightly theirs, and tears for me to have the opportunities that I've been given.

Tip!
When doing half a day of fasting, or even 24 hours, choose to abstain in the morning. You have already gone the whole night without food and water and are already in a fasted state; think about the word 'break-fast'. Perhaps if you just drink water and herbal teas all day and have a normal dinner, then you have actually achieved 24 hours relatively easily.

I tend to organise my fasting day when I have the opportunity to have an extended meditation practice in the morning (so that I can experience hunger during meditation), and then keep myself busy until dinner. The more you sit around thinking about how hungry you are, the hungrier you become!

The Old Jo

It hasn't always been health foods and fasting for me, as in what feels like my previous life I went out partying for days at a time, pummelling my poor body with copious amounts of drugs and alcohol. I remember one weekend when a top DJ came to the small Thai island I was living on, and who played at different venues on three consecutive nights. On the first night, which happened to be a Friday, I ate a lot of ecstasy tablets, then took valium to get to sleep. After sleeping all day I then woke up and had a line of cocaine to get me going and into the shower, continuing to shovel this rubbish up my nose all night until the sun came up. Again more valium to sleep, up again in the evening with more marching powder to get me out the house and onto the dance floor where I took a combination of ecstasy, cocaine and alcohol all of that night and the whole of the next day (I chain-smoked throughout the whole weekend too). I didn't get home until the Monday night, plus I'd hardly eaten anything all weekend.

When I look back on what I was doing to myself it scares me, but at the time I thought I was having 'fun'. Back then I was doing all I knew how to, but now of course I can see that it was destructive and damaging. I am hugely grateful for my new perspective and the only ecstasy in my life now is my newfound freedom, my years of hedonism gone forever.

I'm sure you can find something in your life that you are grateful for: children, family and a roof over your head, even if life is tough. There is always someone worse off than ourselves, and there is beauty in nature if we cannot find it in our own lives.

Gratitude Bears Fruit

When we are in a place of gratitude, rather than feeling like a victim and sorry for ourselves, we expand rather than contract. Gratitude is a seed and, therefore, catalyst for more of the same to grow. We are saying YES to life rather than no, and we can quite literally change direction through gratitude.

Quantum Gratitude

Now we are going into the future and generating a state of gratitude for something that hasn't happened yet. Picking something from our vision board and imagining that it is already happening, we transport ourselves there. We've already talked about the chemical reaction in our brain when we do this, which then gets delivered into our body. We are changing just from the thought, and if we think it enough then we actually become it, our external landscape *catching up* with our mind-set.

- We feel grateful that our wonderful new mate is in our lives, we feel so loved, so accepted, so nurtured
- We are grateful for the enhanced relationships with our family members
- We are grateful for this new insight in our lives
- We are grateful for our meditation practice which we can see already is changing everything in our lives
- We are grateful for our amazing job
- We are grateful for the sound sleep we are having

- We are grateful for the healthy food we feed ourselves

EXERCISE THIRTEEN: **The Gratitude Journal**
This is a wonderful daily exercise that I advise you do in the evening when you get into bed. I have a different journal for the evening that lives in my bedside cabinet and I highly recommend you do the same thing.
Each day write down what you are grateful for, starting with the words: **I am grateful for:**

- Firstly write down all of the things that actually happened to you that you are grateful for. For example: I am grateful for my morning meditation; I am grateful for my children; I am grateful for my husband who smiled at me this morning; I am grateful for my dog who took me for a wonderful walk; I am grateful for a lovely lunch with my friend, etc.

- Then do your 'quantum gratitude' practice, and write about all the things that are going to happen in the future as if they already have happened (seeing as the quantum field does not know the difference between what has actually happened and what is a visualisation). It will look something like this: I am grateful for my amazing new job which I love so much; I am grateful for the bottomless energy that I have felt all day; I am grateful for the superfoods that I have eaten all day; I am grateful for my bank account holding more money than it ever has before, etc.

Try and list at least five things in each category *every day*. What is amazing about this practice is that it gets easier and easier everyday to find things to be grateful for because we have begun the process of LOOKING and becoming aware of them.

Optional extra: Once I have listed all the things I am grateful for I also list any quantum magic that I've witnessed in my day, like a conversation that I am so pleased I had, or my friend phoning me just as I was thinking of them.
Added to that I then write down three intentions for the next day, just to plant those seeds of potential in my brain before I go to sleep. The dream state is fertile ground for these seeds to germinate ready for sprouting the next day.

MEDITATION SEVEN: Gratitude Meditation
Get settled in your meditation space and make sure you will not be disturbed.

Set your timer into five equal times (if you have 25 minutes to practise you want five lots of five minutes), get comfortable and close your eyes.

1st Fifth:
Become aware of your breathing and start to step back from your thoughts, becoming the observer. Watch what comes through, with no judgement, simply witnessing each thought. Do they come from the past or future? Are they thoughts of planning? Remembering? Or worrying? Keep coming back to the present moment.

Follow your breath all of the way in, and all of the way out, using it to *rest* your mind upon. Up until now our meditations have been very visual with a story to follow, but this time we are going to simply use the breath.
So when you realise that you have disappeared into a

thought, bring yourself back to your inhale and exhale.
Over and over again.

2nd Fifth:

Then start to concentrate only on the exhalation, for
this is where we let go. For the first few breaths you can
exhale through your mouth, even making a sound if you
wish. Really have the sense that you are releasing. Then
come back to regular nasal breathing but still with your
attention on the exhale.

Now imagining that there is smoke coming out of your
nose as you exhale, and this smoke carries all of the guilt,
blame, remorse, shame, anger and addictive tendencies
with it. Enjoy letting them go. Continue doing this until
your next bell sounds.

3rd Fifth:

Now we are going to switch to the inhalation and breathe
in forgiveness and love. Everything is going to be ok.
The universe forgives you, your best friend the quantum
field forgives you, so you must forgive yourself. Now is
the time, breathe in LOVE. You are loved unconditionally
by the quantum field, it is there for you always, listening
and waiting for your command. Obeying your every
wish, because wishes DO come true. You are setting
yourself free. Breathe forgiveness into every pore of your
body, not just at your nose; feel that every single cell is
receiving love. Continue doing this until the next bell
rings.

4th Fifth:

Then we are going to put the two sections together,
breathing OUT struggle and pain and breathing IN
forgiveness and love. In this way we begin to realise that

EVERY SINGLE BREATH becomes an opportunity for growth. And even if we have missed many opportunities before now to change and become a better person, we are here now, ready to let the past go. Say to yourself: *'From this moment on I move only forwards on my journey.'*

Once you feel that you've got this, let go of the visualisation and enjoy the Zero Point. This is it, this is balance, there is nothing holding us back now. Remain here until your timer chimes, but continue to stay in this state for the rest of the day. How long can you maintain it? The more we practise the longer we are able to; this is why we meditate.

Concluding Fifth:

Lastly we are going to think of something or someone that we are grateful for. It can be your child, wife, house, parents, spiritual connection, pet, anything at all. And begin to get to know this feeling; where is it in your body; what does it feel like; and how easy is it to find? Then once you have it start to expand it, open yourself up to it, surrender to the emotion. Can you fill your whole body with it? And then expand it even further? Continue to do this generation of gratitude to include other people and experiences. Can you see that everything, even difficulty, is there to teach us something. Everything is exactly as it's supposed to be. There are no mistakes, only learnings. Can you feel gratitude for it all?

Once your timer sounds see if you can hold on to this gratitude and take it into your day seeing how every person, conversation, event and thought that you have is a message from your subconscious mind: are you picking this information up?

Generosity

Gratitude opens the door for generosity, for when we feel abundant it is easier to give to others that which we already have. Generosity is the other side of the gratitude coin. We can't give altruistically from a place of lack, so we must work on this initial stage first so that we may reach a position where we can give unconditionally. When we give to others we give first to ourselves, as we've already discussed in several chapters (think the 'selfish Buddhas'). Look at these two examples:

1. A person who lives in lack and gives nothing: they are of course attracting the same energy to themselves and will always live a life of shortage whether that is of money, love, friendship or in depression. They are closed down emotionally and spiritually.

2. A person who gives what they do not need: immediately they are attracting back to them more of everything because they have opened themselves up to limitlessness and will always have enough themselves.

A Lesson From The Beggar

I went to India for the first time in 2005 and although I instantly fell in love with the country, the deprivation, the way so many lived and the number of beggars deeply upset me. In the guidebooks that I read before I arrived it stated categorically not to give to the beggars as it only encouraged them further. So I began my Indian journey saying *'bas'* a lot (Hindi for *'that's enough'*) as I'd been advised to.

Then I met up with a friend of mine in the Himalayas and she asked me why I didn't give to any of the beggars when she was giving freely to them.

'You're not supposed to,' I replied, *'It encourages them.'*

I dutifully regurgitated from the guidebook.

'Then you are closing down your opportunity to be generous,' she answered.

And in that moment something clicked, two neurons that had never connected before did so right there and then. I got it! Generosity unifies two people in a beautiful joining of souls, and why would I not want to offer a few rupees, which to them is a lot and to me is not. It was one of those life lessons that I will never forget and that I am eternally grateful to my friend for.

Generosity, just like all of the other Quantum Qualities, are muscles that need flexing and training to become strong and effortless. Some will be easier to introduce than others, but in time they will all become second nature. And the beauty of this is that you will know that you're getting somewhere because your life transforms becoming satisfying, happy and full of joy.

Smugness

Have you noticed how good it feels when you do something for somebody else? The feeling of smugness that cascades through your whole being? Why don't we do that more often? Why don't we make a point of doing it all the time, why don't we start from today?

I love that feeling and it has an amazing effect on the chemicals in your body, because as soon as your brain registers that you have given to another being you are sending a chemical message that you are a good person, that you are so FULL. That permeates every single cell in your body and you feel enough.

Meditation As Gratitude To Mind

The common thread throughout this book is meditation.
For me it is the ultimate proclamation of gratitude to
my mind. When I make space for it in my day I feel at
peace and I carry the connection around with me all
day. If I forget or don't have time I notice it; my day is
problematic. So much so that I have created a whole new
morning routine, that you've read about already, to ensure
that it is the very first thing and priority of *every* day no
matter what is on my schedule. The present moment is a
gift, that is why it's called THE PRESENT, and we should
strive to live our lives there as much as possible.

Nutrition as Gratitude to Body

During my hedonistic days I gave very little regard to
what I ate; food was just something that I had to consume
to stay alive, and most of the time I would have a
cigarette to quell hunger pangs. I didn't really enjoy food
back then, but now nothing could be further from that
old truth. I love food, and providing my body and mind
with nutritious substance has become a new passion of
mine.

We fuel our bodies with food, and feed our brains
nutrients. What better way of showing gratitude for these
amazing machines than by giving them high vibrational
nourishment.

Yoga as Gratitude to Mind and Body

Yoga is a wonderful practice to keep the body strong, flexible and balanced as well as preparing the mind for meditation.

'My body is my temple and asanas are my prayers'

This is a famous quote from B.K.S. Iyengar, the founder of Iyengar yoga, which is one of the main lineages initially brought to the west. And why wouldn't we look after this temple of ours? Why treat it with such little respect; I know that I abused my body for the whole of my adult life up until 2012, at aged 40, when I decided that enough was enough.

For more on yoga and nutrition see the final part of this book called the 'How To Get Your Vibe High – The Helpers' (p.221), where I talk about what I have personally used to gain balance in all areas of my life.

REFLECTION: **What Are You Grateful For Right Now?**
If you haven't yet done the first exercise in this chapter then close your eyes right now and think about three things that you are grateful for. Say out loud: 'I am grateful for…' at the beginning of each one.
Journal around what you feel and what emotions this brings up.

Questions and Answers: **Gratitude**

Q: I find it near enough impossible to be grateful for something that hasn't happened yet. Can you help?
A: It will take practice and initially you will have to 'trick'

your mind into this technique, but please persevere as there are so many rewards to reap from doing this.

Q: I hate the word smug, is there another I can use instead?
A: Many of our American members have told me how much they dislike this word and what negative connotations it holds in the USA. In the UK it is not so negative I think, and I'm sorry if it upsets/triggers you. What I mean by it is when you do something and feel really good about it, so perhaps you could use 'contented' instead. Or another word that makes you feel extremely good about yourself.

Time to move on to our very last Quantum Quality.

Quantum Quality Eight
Trust

*Now that the seeds of intention have been sown
we can sit back and watch them grow*

To reach a place where we have no resistance to the
ups and downs of life is our ultimate goal. We learn to
swim with the current of adversity without it pulling us
under; we become strong and unfaltering no matter what
challenges us.

It is not what happens to you, *but how you respond to it*.
It's not that we are getting to a place where bad things no
longer happen, rather we have grown so much that those
bad things slide off us, like water off a duck's back.
Trust is similar to acceptance, but here we take it slightly
further as we *surrender* to life completely. However, it
is imperative that the other seven qualities have been
embraced first because if we haven't connected to our
true self, *our inner wisdom*, then we may be surrendering
to the wrong thing.
Can you see how each of the Quantum Qualities leads
on to the next, some of them with subtle and valuable
variations:

1. **Awareness** to see where we are, and that it is
   possible to change
2. **Unlearning** our societal conditioning and
   discovering who we *really* are underneath it
3. **Forgiving** everything that we've done in the

past, which will set us free so that we can move
forwards and experience **Love** of self

4. **Acceptance** of the flow of life; go with it rather
   than against it, and begin to feel FULLness
5. **Quantum Jumping** into the life that we deserve,
   now that we realise that we are enough
6. **Perspective** to see things as they really are, rather
   than how we perceive them to be
7. **Gratitude** for all that we already have and will
   have in the future
8. **Trust:** Only once here are we able to fully
   surrender to our experience with no resistance

When all fight, fear, inner conflict and struggle have been
released and we feel space opening up instead, then we
are ready to truly trust our quantum partner. Suddenly
our mind is free from worrying about saying a mean
word or having another drink, for you simply no longer
have to do that.

I can think back to when I was 'trying' to stop drinking
and my whole day was filled with either thoughts of
how much I hated myself for drinking so much the
night before, or fear of how much I was going to drink
later that day and what I was going to say or do. There
was no room for anything else, no room for any magic.
Hopefully, however, now that you are at this point
you have seen a glimpse of what is possible and what
freedom looks like as well as how to get there. When
you have 'let go' of the destructive emotions that were
ruining your life, your mind opens up to a vast clear sky
with magical stars twinkling with future promise. Once
you have surrendered to what is possible and opened the
door to the unlimited possibilities that surround you, you
will begin to experience life like never before.

Resistance As A Teacher

When resistance appears it is giving you a message that something is out of balance, so rather than dismissing it delve in deeper to find out the root of the problem. Change can bring about a whole load of resistance because we are being asked to expand, walk away from our familiar reality and go beyond what we know and feel is safe. But at some point we are going to have to take that step, *the leap of faith*, and if you have worked through the Quantum Qualities then you are indeed ready to jump into your new life.

When resistance emerges take a step back, give it space, and see why it is there. This whole programme is about SPACE to see reality as it is, not just how it has always appeared to be.

No More Worry

Can you imagine a life with no resistance? Where you trust that everything that is there is meant to be? You were supposed to miss the train so that you could take an important telephone call; you are stuck in traffic so that you are not personally involved in the accident up ahead; if you had squeezed yourself into that lift you would not have had the chance meeting with your friend who was in the next one, etc.

Worry is such a waste of our energy, it gets you nowhere other than on anxiety medication. As an experiencer of Post-Traumatic-Stress Disorder (PTSD), after a speeding motorbike drove into my stationary car and the driver was taken unconscious to hospital, I can talk first-hand of the worry of driving after the accident. The hours I have spent driving, and as a passenger in a car, truly believing that I was not going to survive the journey. This left me feeling exhausted, tense, anxious, nervous, and the worry in my brain sending chemicals to my body translating to white knuckles, a quickened heart rate and contraction on every level. Yet I did live through each subsequent journey, and what I put my mind and body through every time was for nothing because I am OK. I survived.

What I had done was hardwired my brain to believe the memory of the accident was real each time I got in a car. I had to UNlearn that memory and make a new one; that driving is safe. Today I love driving again having released the old patterns of the worry and stress of PTSD.

Can you see how worry is a waste of time and energy, when we could be getting on with something more productive in life? Once we let go of the old patterns and learn that trust is the key, we open the door to true beauty, to a higher vibration. And just like a mobile phone mast towers over the area for all the local people to connect with it, a signal is beaming out as we begin to manifest vaster, wider and more exceptional experiences than ever before.

The Magic Faraway Tree
When I was a child I was fascinated by the collection of stories set in The Magic Faraway Tree. If you are not familiar with them, the tree is located in a forest and a group of children discover it one summer. When they climb to the top (meeting strange folk along the way) they see that the top of the tree is enshrouded in cloud. They then realise that there is a magical land that lives in the clouds, and each time they visit it has changed and they have amazing adventures in unusual environments. Perhaps Enid Blyton knew on some level about the quantum world, and I know now why it struck such a chord with me more than 30 years ago.

Quantum Knows Best

Let go, let life take you where you are supposed to go because when we think we know where we should be going we miss out on the magic. And if we limit ourselves to only what we've experienced before, then we put the brakes on our potential future. The quantum is unlimited and we are connected to everything in it, and if we believe that anything is possible, it will bring us more than we've ever known before. We have to trust that the quantum is going to provide what is perfect for our individual, unique requirements. We do not have to know the 'how', just the 'what', and then believe in the magic.

MEDITATION EIGHT: The Lake

Get comfortable in your spot, close your eyes, relax the mind and bring your attention to the breath. Watch your breath come in and out without being too fixed. There is a fine line between being relaxed as we watch the journey of the breath, and being stuck on or in it; it should be a light attention.

With time you will begin to notice 'gaps' opening up in between thoughts; moments of emptiness, and this is when you have stepped out onto the quantum field of possibilities; this is where we want to visit as much as possible. Keep coming back to the breath over and over again, steadying and stabilising the mind.

Now imagine a large beautiful lake surrounded by mountains.

This is a magical lake of pure potentiality, and contains everything that you have ever desired; all of your wishes and all of your dreams. It is your lake. Approach it and sit down at its shore. Notice as much detail about your lake as you can; colour of the water, foliage, if there are ripples, waves or if it is completely still. What can you hear? Smell? What is the temperature around your lake? Then put your hand in and find out if it is cool or warm water.

Because this is your lake you can have all that it contains. Think about what you believe around your addiction in this very last meditation. Look back to where you were in the beginning, when you first picked up this book; perhaps scared; sceptic; playing a smaller game than you are now. Look at the lake and know that in it you are the person that you have always wanted to be; content; happy; healthy; and abundant in every way. You can have that if you want it.

Next you are going to get a cup and fill it with water from the lake and pour the water over you head. What does unlimited potential feel like? The water is reaching every part of you, and maybe you'd now like to fill the cup up again and drink the water. Feel the water on the inside as well as the outside of you.

You may be able to go into this last stage immediately the first time you do this meditation, or you may like to work your way up to it.

It's time to jump or dive in to the lake and claim what is rightfully yours. A happy life is waiting for you. A sober life is waiting for you. A healthy life is waiting for you. And if you do not claim what is waiting for you in your lake then no one else will, because this lake is yours and no ones else's. It has been sitting here the whole of your life unclaimed until now, and will continue to do so if you do not believe that you deserve it. No one else will ever be able to even visit this lake. When you dive in you join with your ultimate potential, you accept, you believe and you trust yourself. Swim around and revel in this experience for as long as you can today....

When your timer goes or you feel ready to let go of the lake visualisation, come back to the breath. Don't worry – it is your lake and you can visit it again anytime you want to. Stabilise your mind on the breath following it in and out and reflect on how you feel now compared with at the beginning of the meditation.

Quantum Gratitude

So for us to manifest exciting *new* experiences we have to be grateful for our future relationships, job, health etc. We know that the mind doesn't know the difference between what has already happened and what is in the future, so we must expand our minds and include being grateful *before* our dreams become fact. The more we trust the process, the easier it becomes.

Intuition

What we have been doing throughout this book is connecting to our intuition. We have the answers already within us, and now need to trust them. When we retreat from our outer environment and slow down enough to hear our wise words of wisdom that come from deep within us, then we have solved our life riddle; it all becomes clear and we trust ourselves wholly. No one else can give you YOUR answers, as like a snowflake we are all unique, this is your journey with your own exclusive set of trials and tribulations to master.

And when we solve the puzzle it is like coming home, and as you look back at all the stupid things you've done you smile, as you know you could never go back there. Prison or freedom: that is what you are choosing with every belief, attitude, thought, word and action that you take. It is only your responsibility to do this and you can no longer blame anyone else.

Do You Get It Yet?

Has it clicked for you how we have been living our lives

back to front for so long? How we *know* that if we have chapped lips we've either been out in harsh weather or are dehydrated; how if we have a broken leg there was an accident to get it that way. So why do we *not* ask *why* we have a certain dis-ease or illness? Why do we not wonder why some people *always* get the cold that's doing the circuit, yet others *never* do? And why don't we look at the cause of our over-drinking, over-eating or destructive over-anything?

What Is Your Why?
It didn't happen for no reason. Yet society seems to want us to think like that, but I hope this book has sparked the *'why'* question in you. I hope you will begin to peel away the layers of what you've always thought and ask yourself 'Is that really true?'
The Buddha gave teachings and told his students,

'Don't just blindly believe me, go and find out for yourself if what I have told you is true'

Don't believe everything that you are being told; go and find your own truth; your own happiness; your purpose and find peace with yourself. Get yourself support while you go through this process with a community of people who will lift you up, not bring you down and question why you are becoming free. And be warned that not everyone is there yet, and you are going to come across people who will not want to see you fly, and they will try and clip your wings so that you stay small with them. And it's hard to let go of relationships, jobs, family members and places that you've been hanging out in for years perhaps. But if they are going to lure you backwards then you may have to do this in the beginning as you steady yourself in your new world.

What are the causes to your effect? Do the exercises in this book to find out your why, your set-point, where exactly your pendulum is swinging. Then find out why, because if you don't do this; don't look for the reasons you are where you are then you can never be fully free. Once you shine light on the darkness and keep the light on, by meditating every day, you walk fully into your potential liberation from all suffering.

Living Life 'On Purpose'
A fabulous side effect of this connection to self and, therefore, your intuition is that you will naturally find your purpose in life. Old ways of doing things just will not do any longer as the 'shoulds' of life fall away and what makes you feel alive is the only 'job' you can partake in. This can be a scary time for many as they realise that they are wasting their precious human life in a relationship which is harming them, or a career which is unfulfilling. Suddenly before they know it they've handed in their notice and retrained in their passion; I see this with my clients all of the time and it's what I did too. When I left my sensible London job after 12 years in the same building everyone said to me,

'You're so brave, Jo!'

But what I was feeling inside was,

'Get me out of here! I'm suffocating! I know there is more to life than this!'

Now I'm not saying that you must pack your job in and get a divorce, only warning you that the clearer you get about who you are and what you want, the more the universe will provide you with just that.

We are CONSTANTLY manifesting with every single belief, attitude, thought, word and action. It's happening whether we like it or not. You have changed dramatically since the beginning of this book, since waking up this morning, even in the last five minutes. So make it all worth it, manifest consciously the life that you want rather than unconsciously repeating the same problems over and over again.

And if like me and so many of my clients before, you suddenly realise that anything is possible and get one of those wonderful 'Aha' moments then please let me know. I LOVE to hear when it happens!

I believe that we all have a purpose for being on this planet, with some having found what makes their soul sing already whilst others continue their search. Stick with meditation and all will become clear, as the deeper you go within yourself the closer to your true calling you get.

Paying It Forward

What is really exciting about taking this path is that you give the green light for others to do the same. They see you doing it, they watch you grow into the best version of yourself that you can be, and they raise themselves up also: your children, your family, friends, colleagues and acquaintances. Everyone jumps on board and we walk the path of freedom together. For we are the next generation of leaders who will be bringing the people in our lives with us; have the motivation to get free not just for your own salvation but so that you can support the next wave of individuals ready to walk this path.

I know for me the ride of life has been dramatic, that the lows I've felt and now the highs of freedom cannot *not* be shared; I have to climb to the top of the mountain and shout as loudly as I can the method to become free.

And there is so much room up here on this mountain, so please come and join me and enjoy the fantastic view.

Intentions Are Seeds

Where do you want to be? What seeds are you planting? Act in line with your intended outcome, rather than where you currently are. Change the intention = change the reality. Beliefs become intentions, intentions become emotions and we act upon our emotions. Whichever one is the strongest is going to win, so which of your beliefs are the strongest? Where are you putting your energy? For this is what you are creating. And once you can see this clearly and put out strong positive beliefs, intentions and emotions, then you can trust that the quantum will take care of the process; that bit is not your job.

Now that the seeds of intention have been sown we can sit back and watch them grow

This is a tricky part of the process as it's here that we must LET GO and allow the quantum to do its work. Just like once you have planted your seeds in the soil you do not make them sprout and grow, so too must you let the quantum germinate your intentions. And it will do its utmost to form the most magnificent creation, so be very careful what you wish for and don't be surprised if what you receive back is not quite what you expected. For sometimes our minds cannot envision the big picture and what we are gifted is far more amazing than we could have ever imagined, so make space for that to happen.

EXERCISE FIFTEEN: **A Day In The Life Of Trust**
What could your life look like if you took away all of the worry and trusted that everything was going to be ok?

Start with small events in the beginning and then work up to more substantial actions.

Here are some examples to get you started:

- The very first trust, first thing in the morning, will be that we have had enough sleep the night before to get us through this new day
- I trust that there are no coincidences; every conversation that I am privy to and person that I come into contact with is there for a reason. I am open to the messages that are all around me; I hear them and act upon them
- I trust that I wasn't supposed to catch the train that I just missed, whatever the reason it is the right one
- I trust that the disagreement that I had with somebody is teaching me something that I need to know about myself
- I trust that when I drive to the store I will get a parking space right outside the main door
- Now add your own....

Collective Quantum Consciousness

As I write this book whilst in retreat I have watched the Scottish weather change quite distinctively as different groups have come and gone from the centre. It began with a Tai Chi assemblage who manifested, as a group, sunny spells with no rain. Then the day that they left we had thick fog roll in from the sea, which lasted for the two days with me as the only guest; so along with the island residents (around 10 people) that was my manifestation, and boy was it ethereal. As I wrote about creating unlimited possibilities in this book, the words were jumping off the page and manifesting right in front of my eyes as pure magic. We lived for two days in this fog, or heaven on earth as I viewed it, and speaking to someone who has lived at the retreat for over 15 years, he said he had never seen anything quite like it before. Then two groups arrived together, a total of 30 people, and the fog vanished instantly, in its place it became overcast with sunny spells.

I truly believe that the group energies were having an effect on the weather, as everything that we put 'out there' comes back again; it has to; that is the job of the quantum. Perhaps there was a collective expectation of cloud in autumnal Scotland? It has been so very interesting to watch, every second feeling like a miracle; and this is what happens when we gift ourselves time to retreat, time to watch, time to become the ultimate observer.

And what I was witness to in this ultimate observer role was beyond thought and 'self', for I became observer to both the object (thoughts) AND subject (self). Giving yourself the gift of releasing the physical world (0.00001%) and connecting to what is beyond (99.99999% energy) will blow your mind and change your life forever.

Plugging in to limitlessness, being able to let go of the world of form and trusting in the part of you that is formless, nameless, pure love and acceptance, is what this approach is about. So much more than addiction, this is a way of life and once you have transcended the substance and reason you are reading this book, you will discover that the QS system you are learning can be applied to *everything* in your life.

Tip!
We can all trust, it's not something that we have to learn to do but we do have to decide what we are going to put our trust in. Trust is like a computer; what you program

in you get out, so if you trust that you are going to find sobriety difficult then you've just made that decision and the computer will return to you exactly what you requested; struggle. Yet it's all already there, every possibility, so what are you going to choose to trust? Bringing Trust into each of the Quantum Qualities:

- **Awareness** – I TRUST I am in the right place
- **Unlearning** – I TRUST my own unique truth
- **Forgiveness & Love** – I TRUST my heart from now on
- **Acceptance** – I TRUST the flow of life
- **Alternate Realities** – I TRUST my dreams will come true
- **Perspective** – I TRUST that when my alarm goes off I've had enough sleep
- **Gratitude & Generosity** – I TRUST there is always enough

---

REFLECTION: **Turning Our Lives Upside Down**
Look at the opposite meaning of some of the words I have used in this book and see how we are turning our lives inside out and around 180 degrees. Quantum Sobriety is about doing things differently:

FROM = **TO**
Fear = **Love**
Resistance = **Surrender**
Struggle = **Effortlessness**
Problem = **Ease**
Difficulty = **Comfort**
Worried = **Relaxed**
Destruction = **Construction**
Limited = **Unlimited**
Blame = **Acceptance**
Blocked = **Flow**

You get my point. We are turning our lives around if we choose to, and if we believe that we can. What do you believe? Where do you want to live from, which side of the above chart?

Questions and Answers: **Trust**

Q: You talk about the ultimate observer but I don't really know what you mean.

A: What we see is like a picture on the TV screen. We know that the picture is not the intelligence; that is coming from the DVD player/TV/projector. The images are passing across the screen and are the result of the movie that has already been made months, if not years ago. So our thoughts are like the pictures on the screen, our minds and bodies are like the DVD player/TV/projector, and ultimate reality is like the room/house/planet that it is being watched in.

We limit ourselves by believing that we are merely the movie and DVD player, for we are much more than that.

Q: I like the idea of resistance dropping but I've never experienced that myself, what is it like?

A: Relief! So much struggle is released at the moment that we finally 'get' trust. We realise that it is so futile and exhausting to keep striving to 'be' somewhere else, when we could relax into exactly where we are already. It is not about the destination; it's the journey. And we've heard this saying a thousand times, but think about it; we are *meant* to be exactly where we are right in this moment. So trust that fact, and let go of everything else.

Now at the very end of the eight Quantum Qualities, do you feel ready and prepared for the future of your dreams? Perhaps before anything else you need to have a plan of action as to how you are going to put all of this information together and into your unique situation. That is where we are going next.

The Plan
Putting It All Into 'Practice'

Observe that you are not travelling into your future, rather, the future is moving towards you

Preparation

It's hugely important to get yourself ready for situations where you would normally drink/eat/binge, as if you are not prepared it will be much easier to get pulled back into the past. It's time to think about exactly what you are going to say in certain situations: in the pub, at a party, on holiday, etc. The first few times you go out and find yourself in difficult circumstances are going to be the biggest challenge and once you get yourself through them, each subsequent situation will get easier and easier.

You know why you are doing this; you've done the meditations, and understand better the underlying reasons that got you to this point. And you trust yourself; you know that you are about to embark on the most exciting adventure ever: the journey *within*. You know that it is going to make your life so much more wonderful, but there is going to be an initial period of adjustment.

So now preparation is everything. What are you going to do instead of eating the whole kitchen cupboard or opening the wine when the kids drive you mad? What are you going to order at the pub when you next go? What are you going to do in the evenings from now on if you usually spend the last section of the day drunk?

Some suggestions follow but this really is very personal and you must think: What am I going to enjoy? It's no good writing down 'yoga' just because it sounds like a really good thing to do but you know you won't stick to it. Be realistic; what do you *enjoy* doing?

- Meditate
- Do some Yoga/Swimming/Tennis/Badminton/Any Exercise
- Make a smoothie (more about food in the next section)
- Read a book
- Do some gardening
- Journal about your feelings
- Paint/Draw
- Go for a walk
- Dance
- Have a bath
- Meditate (yes I have put it twice!)

I have clients that have started having three baths a day in the beginning to get out of their bad habit, and a month or so down the line they switched back to just one bath a day. Obviously I would say meditation is the best thing to do, *which is why it appeared twice,* because you are creating a good habit at the same time as ridding yourself of a destructive one.

Say What?

This applies mainly to the drinkers amongst you, for when you stop over-eating or eliminate sugar from your diet there is not going to be too much objection from those around you (if you have some great healthy recipes that is). However the same is not true for alcohol, and you will need to be armed and ready with a reason for not drinking the poison.

'Oh go on, John, just have one.'

'You not drinking tonight, Theresa? Why ever not? Here have a glass of this.'

'Come on, Bob, we're celebrating.'

'I know you're not driving, Elaine, so come on, join me.'

You have to have a really good reason, and stay totally resolute when drinkers start arguing with you. And it will be all of their 'stuff' – the fact that you are strong enough to not drink and they are not will make them feel threatened, which is why some cannot bear the thought of you not having a drink. It's sad but true. These are some white lies that you can tell:

- I'm driving tonight
- I'm taking antibiotics
- I'm working tomorrow
- I've got a really early start tomorrow
- I'm not very well
- I'm pregnant (that's obviously not going to work for everyone!)

Sometimes you can get away with these but they have get out clauses for the drink-pushers because they are not ultimately true,

Them: *'Go on have a drink.'*

You: *'I can't, I'm driving.'*

Them: *'Don't worry about that, Sue is driving, get a lift with us!'*

Tell The Truth?

When I say this I know it horrifies many of you, as your over-drinking could well be totally unknown to friends and family, or even a secret that you've kept from everyone for years. I get that, and so use the excuses above; I wouldn't even class this as a real lie in these circumstances for you are bettering yourself through doing so.

But if you are up for it then say,

'I've had a problem with drinking and I've stopped. Please support me.'

Someone would be very out of order if they still tried to get you to drink after hearing that.

By being honest it does get others to think about their own drinking,

'Did you see Terry at the party tonight? He's stopped drinking, and I really admire him. I wish I had the strength to do that.'

Obviously if you're not comfortable with this then that's fine (many of my clients are not and many have joined the online forum under a pseudonym), but you must be prepared before the event arrives. Think ahead for the next few months at what social occasions you have planned, and then do the exercises below for the events that you *know* you are going to encounter.

EXERCISE SIXTEEN: Get Prepared!
Make a list of at least five activities that you are going to do instead of drink/eat/smoke/shout:

1.
2.
3.
4.
5.

Then make a further list of what you are going to say

when asked why you are not drinking/eating sugar/
smoking:

1.
2.
3.
4.
5.

MEDITATION NINE: 10,000 Cords

This is a very powerful meditation from the Chocolate
Shaman if you need to change your energy quickly. So if
you are feeling angry, negative, triggered or lost then you
can do this visualisation. Get on your cushion, set your
timer and close your eyes.

Come to the breath, or sound, it's up to you, whichever
you feel most connected to in this moment (just don't
switch between the two in any one meditation), and stay
here for between two and 10 minutes depending on how
long you have. Watch the breath come in and out / notice
sounds far in the distance and then the ones that are
closer.

Notice that from left to right in a half circle in front of
you there are 10,000 golden cords with one end of each
lying at your feet. They then run away from you as far as
you can see off over the horizon. Each one is a different
potential and right now there are 10,000 different
alternate realities available to you. Look down and you
will see that one of these cords is attached to you at your
belly area; this is your current reality.

Pull the cord out and place it on the floor with all of the
others. Then take a look from left to right and notice
which reality out of all of the 10,000 possibilities is the
most attractive to you; there will be one of these cords

that is pulsating with the highest vibrational energy imaginable right now and this one is able to give you everything that you have ever dreamt of, and more.

If you are ready then pick up the end of that cord and attach it to yourself. Feel the power, intention, happiness, laughter, good health, success, sobriety, ideal weight, positivity, great relationships, prosperity, peace of mind and everything else that you could wish for. What does it feel like to meet an alternative you? Revel in this new energy...

Observe that you are not travelling *into* your future, rather, the future is moving *towards you*. Once you have sown the seeds of intention, there isn't anything that you need to do other than sit back and watch them grow.

When you are ready, let go of the visualisation BUT keep hold of the vibration of it. Come back to your breath/sound, whichever you have been using during this meditation. Gently begin to move your body, bring your hands together in a prayer position at your chest, look down with your eyes still closed to your chest, and thank yourself for making it to the end of the book and the last meditation. Thank yourself for believing that you deserve the best, deserve to be happy, and that you will permanently remain in this certainty.

EXERCISE SEVENTEEN: **Making A Commitment**
The book is nearly finished and you now have all of the tools at hand to create the life of your dreams. It's time to make a commitment or two. Copy this letter out into your journal filling in the gaps that are relevant to you. Add more if you feel that you'd like to.

Dear (insert your name)

Thank you for taking me on this amazing journey within myself, for learning about my superpower, and finally dealing with what (insert your addiction/imbalance) has been covering over all of these years.

I am devoted to helping myself become the best possible me and I know that I deserve this. To stay on track I am making the following commitments:

1. To stop (fill in your addiction) completely
2. To meditate everyday for (fill in the amount)
3. To get support by contacting (fill in which programme/therapist you would like to work with)
4. To do (fill in what type of exercise) (how many times per week) every week.
5. To eat better by including (fill in what foods you are going to introduce into your diet)
6. (add your own)
7. (add your own)
8. (add your own)

I'm so glad I did this, I feel really positive and fired up for the future, not depressed and despairing like I used to be. I know that I deserve to be happy and can feel that my fear has already turned 180 degrees into love!

Signed: (sign your name)
Date: (put today's date)

Tip!
You are now connected to your highest potential reality, your frequency is high, and you are capable of anything.

All you have to do to maintain this is stay connected to your essence/superpower in meditation. Remember to start off with five minutes every day, building slowly up to the optimum amount of 30 minutes daily.

If you can throughout the day close your eyes briefly and come back to the present moment. Take a second to notice the smells, the taste in your mouth, the temperature and sounds around you. Touch your index finger and thumb together on one or both sides as you do this in 'chin mudra' and find the connection to your essence.

Then release and carry on with your day…

REFLECTION: **End Questionnaire**

- How do you feel *right now* about yourself in 3 words:
    1. ....
    2. ....
    3. ....

- How stressed do you feel *right now* on a scale of 1 to 10?
  1 being not stressed and 10 being very stressed:

- How happy do you feel *right now* on a scale of 1 to 10?
  1 being not happy and 10 being very happy:

- List here the top five changes that have taken place since you read the Quantum Sobriety book:

  1. ....
  2. ....
  3. ....
  4. ....
  5. ....

- List here the top five changes that you plan to make now:

  1. ....
  2. ....
  3. ....
  4. ....
  5. ....

- What are you going to do instead of drink/eat/ take drugs?:

  1. ....
  2. ....
  3. ....
  4. ....
  5. ....

We would love to hear from you and for you to enter the results of both your Beginning Questionnaire and End Questionnaire into our private and secure online survey. The more data we receive the clearer the picture becomes of just how transformative Quantum Sobriety is, and will enable QS to be more readily available to those that are ready for it. You can support our work in this way by visiting our website workbook page, where you will find the survey: www.quantumsobriety.com/workbook

Part Three:
How To Get Your Vibe High – The Helpers

Yoga: **Authentic Ecstasy**
Nutrition: **Eat Yourself 'Clean'**
Nutrition: **Chocolate For Breakfast**
Counselling: **Learning To Ask For Help**
Journalling: **Writing It All Down**

This book couldn't be written without a few words on each of these subjects, which have been instrumental to me finding myself and Quantum Sobriety.

They form the rest of my journey that has not already been covered in this book and may fill in the gaps of the story being told. These helpers got me where I am today and I will always be eternally grateful to them…

Yoga:
Authentic Ecstasy

I found myself, yet lost myself all at the same time

Yoga took me into my body so that I could reach my mind, and without it I most definitely wouldn't be where I am today. I owe so much to yoga and the journey it took me on that I wanted to give it its very own chapter.

For so many of us we are disconnected from who we really are, walking around reacting to our external world with no idea even that there is any other way. For me, for a long time I got that connection through the party scene: drug highs and progressive house music lifted me to another plane but this route came with the baggage of late nights, lack of food and catastrophic hangovers. It took me days to recover, to return to myself from the depths of drug desolation, always wondering if it was worth it yet continually taking myself back to that place. I was hooked to the high, searching for the trance-like state that meditation now gives me daily with no hangover and no compromise.

Right from the very first class I got the same connection from yoga that the club music gave me. I found myself, yet lost myself all at the same time. It was exactly what I had been searching for my whole life. I walked up to the teacher at the end and told her that I was going to be a yoga teacher. This was back in 1998 when yoga was still thought of as extremely alternative, but a spark was ignited and I began a beautiful spiritual journey towards freedom.

I then became addicted to this natural high, realising aged 26 that there WAS another way. I'd been partying hard already for nearly 10 years and would continue to do so for another decade, but something that day changed in me. This first class was to be the catalyst towards a lifelong search for deep inner peace and I began to juggle natural and chemical highs.

The hour-long yoga class became a retreat from my external chaos which at the time was the reality of an abusive relationship, unsatisfying job, continued drug abuse and between 20 and 40 cigarettes a day. It gave me a safe place to be me; I didn't have to pretend or impress anyone, just be honest with my body and my mind. Back then I remember thinking that the meditation at the end of each session was a drag; why did we have to do it? Why couldn't we just do more physical postures! However, this is exactly the path of yoga; we start with the physical body and work our way towards the mind, very few go straight to the bull's-eye. Of course in the West most people concentrate on just the exercise element and by doing so they miss the point, the beauty and the potential experience of ultimate reality.

In the end the incongruence of authentic and chemical ecstasy finally became too much of a strain and something had to give. I couldn't cope with the enormous pull from one type of high to another, and the practice was raising my awareness of self so much that I was finally ready to leave behind chemicals once and for all, and pursue yoga in its entirety…

Eight Limbs

The physical postures are just one of eight segments, which are worked through progressively: just as we do with the eight 'Quantum Qualities'. The Eight Limbs of Yoga form part of the foundation of Quantum Sobriety, and are the route I have personally taken.

As we work through the stages our knowledge deepens and we not only begin to feel the difference, but see our external terrain transform from struggle to abundance.

Here is a breakdown of the Limbs, and how if you progress through them in this order you will eventually experience full realisation of self.

Yama:

These are cultural ethical standards to guide you towards a sense of integrity: non-violence; truthfulness; non-stealing; continence and non-coveting.

Basically if we can do good for others we are attracting good to be done back to us.

Niyama:

These are rules of conduct that apply to individual discipline and include: cleanliness; contentment; spiritual austerity; study of the self; and dedication to your faith.

Developing a meditation practice, going to church, saying grace before meals, going for a walk or sitting in contemplation are all examples of how to practice Niyamas.

Asana:

Here is the only one of the eight limbs that Western culture has fully developed. Most people do not even realise that there are another seven sections to this wonderful and full practice.

Through the exercises we develop a habit of discipline and concentration, which can lead us to meditation.

Pranayama:
Prana in Sanskrit means breath, respiration, life, vitality, wind, energy or strength. Ayama means length, expansion, stretching or restraint. Pranayama thus connotes extension of breath and its control, and teaches us the connection between breath, the mind, and the emotions.
Each class includes breathing exercises to either awaken or calm the body and mind.

Pratyahara:
We move now to the 'higher' stages once the first four have helped us gain some control over our personality and brought more awareness into our daily living. Here we make the conscious effort to draw our awareness away from the external world and take the opportunity to step back and take a look at ourselves.
This withdrawal allows us to objectively observe our cravings and addictions, which are interfering with our inner balance.

Dharana:
The yogi then reaches this sixth stage once the body has been cleared by the physical exercises, the mind refined by the breathing exercises, and the senses brought under control. Here we learn how to slow down the thinking process by concentration on a single mental object: a visualisation, a part of the body or a mantra.
We can do a visualisation, body scan or hold our gaze on an external object.

Dhyana:
Very similar to the previous stage, but the seventh level is achieving stillness without a specific focus. The mind is completely quiet and very few thoughts pass through. *It takes time to reach this level of concentration, but is achievable with dedication and practice.*

Samadhi:
Patanjali (who wrote the Yoga Sutras around 2,500 years ago) describes this final stage as a state of ecstasy. The ultimate goal of yoga is enlightenment, something that cannot be bought or possessed, only experienced. Peace is what everyone searches for, and yoga shows a clear path towards reaching self-realisation.

Authentic Ecstasy
I find it truly ironic that Patanjali talks about the search for 'ecstasy' when my own journey has spanned the distance from the chemical to authentic kind, and that the first class A drug that I took was an ecstasy tablet. I speak time and time again about the natural high that I attain in meditation, and that once you experience this and know that it's possible you begin your own journey towards 'Samadhi'.
It's like I always knew it, on some level of consciousness, and spent my whole adult life searching. And after more than 20 years pursuing the meaning of life I am finally at a place where it is no longer about what or where, and there isn't anything else I need to 'do'. Now it is only about being, allowing, observing and trusting.

So if yoga has called you, listen to her request and get yourself on the mat. These days it is so easy to find a class, as yoga booms throughout the western world. But be selective and try out a number of classes before you settle on a teacher who inspires you, and demonstrates in themselves what you are hoping to achieve. It is a sacred relationship and one which is so deeply personal that you often cannot put it into words. What is 'right' for one will repel another, but with the wealth of classes available there really is so much to choose from.

I Can't Do It
Ask any yoga teacher what the most annoying and frequent reason a person gives for not doing yoga, and they are going to say,

'I can't do yoga because I'm not flexible.'
(Every single yoga teacher will say, *'That is the VERY reason you should be doing yoga.'*)

This person has missed the point; yoga is a journey as we have seen from the Eight Limbs. You wouldn't get in your car to go somewhere but then refuse to turn on the ignition because you're not already there!

For me personally I was absolutely rubbish at some aspects of yoga when I started. I used to have very tight hamstrings, and 15 years or so ago I couldn't get anywhere near touching my toes. During my first training course the teacher used to refer to my hamstrings as 'piano wire'. However the more I stretched my physical body the more it opened up to me, until one day I did indeed touch my toes for the first time. The release of energy overflowed from my eyes and I learnt such an important life teaching in that moment: that ANYTHING IS POSSIBLE.

I stored this evidence in my subconscious mind where it fed my beliefs, attitudes, thoughts, words and actions. And it was within a year of that life-changing event that I opened my shop in Thailand called 'Inner Guidance' and became self-employed for the very first time. Up until that point I had always been an employee but my confidence was growing and I have not been an employee since April 2000. And I'd go as far as to say that I believe I am now unemployable! So far down the rabbit hole am I, living my truth, that I just don't fit into others' compartments anymore.

Living On Purpose
I would also say that I believe each one of us has a purpose; a job that they are meant to be doing and that they would love. For me what I do isn't 'work' in the old paradigm sense for it brings me so much joy. I quite literally jump out of bed excited about what the day will bring. Do you?

Do you love your work or is it something that you do to pay the mortgage, keep on top of the bills, and put food on the table? Do you even believe that it's possible to love your work? I can tell you it is. I have gone from daily commute to living the dream, and my route was yoga. Now that I know who I am, I know what makes me happy and I can, therefore, create a dream life. Follow the meditations and exercises in this book and you will have *your* answers too.

We are all brilliant at something. Perhaps you just don't know what that something is yet? Or you don't believe that what you love to do could pay well enough for you to leave your office job? My hope for this book is that by using it, not only will you have tools to stop drinking/eating/binging or shouting, but also an inner strength, knowledge and confidence to manifest your dreams in all areas of your life. The Quantum Sobriety approach works for everything.

Secret Private Party

Although the drugs are long gone, the deep progressive house music remains. However, now I listen to it whilst in the gym and doing yoga, and I still love it. The music takes me to the Zero Point, it speaks to me, drives me, connects me, and the louder the better.

I didn't tell people for a long time about my secret double life: I was a yoga teacher to the outside world, but also enjoyed lifting weights and spinning. I thought people would judge me and think I was a lesser person because I didn't fit into their perception of how a yoga teacher should behave. And I can tell you it's so wonderful to have broken through that obstacle and to not have to hide a part of me anymore.

What you see is what you get with me these days because I am confident, happy and connected to my own truth which is different from anyone else's. I don't need others' approval anymore; wow, that was a big one and I think I could write a whole book on that subject alone.

You Have Been Called

I can see now that I always had this potential but I didn't know it was there before because it was covered over by my conditioning. Just like a seed that begins to grow underground, we don't see it in the beginning but my authentic truth was always there, trying to push to the surface. For some reason I did listen to that inner voice. It took heaps of time, of course, because there weren't half so many books and none of the videos that are now available on the internet, plus I was either too high on drugs or too low coming down from drugs to notice. Times are changing though, just look at yoga. When I started teaching back in 2001 it was something that only 'hippies' did. I was the *only* one teaching back then in my Hertfordshire town, and it was only forward thinking gyms that had yoga classes. Now it is everywhere, and everyone does it. You can find chair yoga, boxing yoga, rave yoga, orgasm yoga (yes honestly!), surf yoga, kids yoga, classes in offices and of course there are multiple classes in every gym now.

Meditation is also on the rise, with 'mindfulness' being the hip word for it currently (it's non-religious and that works for many more people). It's brilliant, more and more people are connecting to their inner worlds and not just outside stimuli. In fact the vibration is rising for our whole planet. Yes there are some awful things happening right now, but I truly believe this is the old world crumbling away so that a new higher consciousness can emerge, just as we have done in this book: become aware; unlearned; forgiven and then created something new. It has to happen within us first for it to be mirrored on the outside, it makes total sense. When you take care of yourself you are sending a green light out to everyone around you to do the same, they can't do it to the same degree without you.

You have been called, right now, because you are ready

Synthetic Lifestyle
In my own experience the synthetic highs are simply not good enough anymore; I want the real thing, and why would anyone go back to something that is killing them (cocaine, ecstasy, cigarettes, alcohol) when there is a healthy alternative?
It's a total no-brainer and I'm sure you agree with me, but what about with food? The next chapter is going to bend your mind around with what you should and shouldn't be eating in our new high-vibe world.

Nutrition:
Eat Yourself 'Clean'

'NO disease, including cancer, can exist in an alkaline environment'
Dr Otto Warburg, 1931 Nobel Prize winner for cancer discovery

In April 2000 I walked into a detox centre in Thailand to attend a yoga class as I had been told that the teacher, Suzy, could potentially train me to be a teacher myself. Little did I know that Spa Samui would become like a second home and the people that I met there remain firm friends for the rest of my life.

The Times rated 'The Spa' as one of the top 50 restaurants in the world, which was ironic seeing as most people who were staying there were fasting for between three and seven days. The food is amazing and totally healthy and was a revelation to me back then. I learnt about juicing, raw food preparation and how the foods that we eat feed our brain, and that one way or another we become what we eat. For the first time in my life I really started to look at my diet. Because I'd always been petite I'd never had to go on a diet or watch what I ate (too much partying, drugging and cigarettes), so the whole concept intrigued me.

Fast-forward 18 years as I write this and I'm married to a 'clean chef' and have learnt the art of truly looking after myself on all levels, which includes the food that fuels me. This journey has been a slow one, gradually changing the quality of produce to arrive where I am now: vegan and gluten, sugar, dairy, grain and all processed foods free.

I eat a diet that enhances how I feel, and it continues to be fine-tuned as I play with what suits me. My palate has changed and no longer hankers after sugary, salty, packaged foods, now choosing fresh, vibrant whole foods that sustain and nourish my body and soul. Of course I sometimes have a 'cheat' meal but these have shifted from takeaways, which made me feel very unwell (what is the point when you really don't enjoy it?) to occasionally having chips with my salad if I'm out.

Food Addiction
There are literally millions of us who are addicted to fast food and sweets. Did you know that sugar is as addictive as heroin and triggers the same response in the brain as cocaine? Yet this drug is available in every household, every shop, every restaurant, at every celebration that we attend and worst of all we 'treat' our children with this deadly substance. Why is one drug allowed but another ridiculed? Why do we as a nation accept sugar but not heroin? It is all part of our brainwashing and the unlearning that we need to detox from. Once we educate our minds and then our bodies to this new aligned information, we realise that it is up to *us* to make our own rules, rather than blindly follow others.

We are living in a new era, one where we take responsibility for our lives, actions, and choices. Don't believe what you see on the TV, in the newspapers, and clever marketing of products that claim to be healthy *(have you ever seen an advert for vegetables?)*.
Make up your own mind! Start a food diary, and decipher which foods are correct for you. When you eat do you

feel tired because you shouldn't. Watch your energy level after your next meal and decide for yourself, did what you just eat *raise* or *lower* your vibration?

The Science Of Nutrition

When we decide to make changes our brain sends a new message down to our cells and the receptor cells behave in a different way.

With repeated exposure to self-hate, however, these cells will have mutated so much that they are not even capable of taking in nutrients from healthy foods. So we must *begin* with a change in mind-set, and only then can we expect our bodies to follow suit and absorb the maximum from nutrient-dense produce (see Candace. B. Pert, PH.D. in the references).

Vegetables For Breakfast

In the UK we have a dreadful custom of toast and cereal for breakfast, literally the worst two dishes we could have first thing. Both are laden with sugar, setting us up to crash and burn throughout the day. Even smoothies are often based upon sugary tropical fruits, which although perceived to be healthy, are really just a sugar bomb too. Are you crashing at 11am in the office once your first sugar rush subsides? Do you then dip into the biscuit tin to top your addiction up? Perhaps you then have a sandwich for lunch; did you know that bread contains sugar? And of course there must be an afternoon snack of cake with a cup of tea. Pudding after dinner, oh yes please!

So you see how our traditional foods do not nourish us, and we wonder why there is a global obesity crisis. It is easy to amend, there are going to be no surprises here: eat natural food, food that has not been processed or messed around with in any way. This is what should be stored in our cupboards. In fact, shopping gets easier because you have fewer aisles to visit! Begin the shift to more fresh produce and less packaged items.

The best breakfast and one I have most days, is a smoothie. This is the ideal way of getting a load of veg packed into a glass, and ramp up your energy post meditation and exercise or before you start work. Ensure you are not making a sugar bomb by balancing vegetables with fruit, we recommend a 80/20 ratio:

Smoothie Recipe For Two People
- Handful of seasonal berries
- Half an apple (different fruit each day for variety)
- 1 pint of nut milk (recipe further down, or coconut milk/water)
- Handful of spinach
- Handful of other leafy green vegetable (different each day for variety)
- ¼ cucumber
- Supplements if you have them (spirulina/chlorella, etc.)
- Blend until smooth

The Express Lane
My husband, aka the 'clean chef' got to healthy eating the opposite way to me. In just two years he completely 'cleaned' up his act going from sugar addict to health freak. When I met him he would eat ice cream after dinner every night followed by a chocolate bar and perhaps a packaged chocolate milk drink. He had never come across 'clean' eating before. We had both put on a bit of weight during our courting days (takeaways, wine, hours spent looking into each others eyes) with me needing to lose around one stone and Dom two or three. I pulled it off first by going 'clean' and reached my target

in a reasonable amount of time, but remember I had been on this path and had the knowledge for a number of years already; it was not a new concept to me. Dom on the other hand was caught up in a lot of old conditioning, especially around his beloved sugar. He really fought the changed diet until we moved to the retreat centre in 2013 and his resistance dropped with him losing over three stone in the first two years we were there.

And then because of this huge shift in mind-set he began to talk about sugar to anyone and everyone. He drove us all mad! But this came from a place of experience and passion for he not only looked better, but felt AMAZING. No one who is carrying an extra few stone is doing their body any favours. Dom looks younger now and *feels* younger too. This should be our primary motivation to get healthier as it is to move beyond our addiction, to *feel* better.

The Sugar Guinea Pig
Food is a huge part of our lives and our programmes, as we all know the saying 'you are what you eat' but I don't think we really take this on board. If we did then why would we even want to purchase (let alone eat) something that has been made in a laboratory and only

contains chemicals? If you take the Quantum Sobriety approach and apply it to your diet then you are easily going to be able to see what needs changing, and change it effortlessly with the right mind-set. However, don't rush into changing everything at once; work first on the main addiction and only move to food when you feel stable in your new sober world.

With sugar I went from eating quite a lot of commercial chocolate to raw energy bars that you can buy in the supermarket. It was a like for like switch and was *easy*. In 2014 I decided to take it even further because I wanted to see what would happen if I cut out *all sugar* for a month. After the month I felt so amazing that I extended the experiment to six months, and then it became permanent, for why would I go back to something that made me feel like rubbish?

Here are the five main changes that I noticed in the initial MONTH of not eating sugar, and that I have maintained years down the line:

1. I suffered with psoriasis in my hairline since a child and it always got worse in winter as soon as the heating went on.
   Now: GONE completely. I've had years of itch-less cold UK winters with no psoriasis whatsoever.
2. I had a large cyst on my chest, which would flare up once or twice a year and was painful and embarrassing.
   Now: GONE completely and never returned. I cannot tell you how amazing that is.
3. I would class myself as a lifelong insomniac, finding it difficult to get to sleep and stay asleep.
   Now: GONE completely. I can now get to sleep immediately and stay asleep, and this has been such a revelation.

4. **Now: I never get colds**.
5. **Now: TWO inches off my waist** within the first month of going completely sugar-free. At the time I didn't need to lose weight and didn't, *but my body has changed shape permanently.*

So you can see that it was a very interesting experiment and one with such positive results that I simply had to continue, it would be crazy not to. But there is a very important point that I must raise now....

I Don't Miss It

Everyone thinks that I must be trying so hard to not eat cake or a chocolate bar, but that's simply not the case because when you apply the Quantum Sobriety approach that we've looked at in close detail already, it's all about your perception.

Yes it took a while to wean myself off, just like all of the other substances I've had addictions to; all having similar initial physical withdrawal symptoms of headache, fatigue and/or sickness, but once you are over that you are left only with the mind cravings.

And the mental addiction will either take you to hell and make life unbearable for you (the old paradigm route), or you can choose freedom. As ever it's up to you, and only you. What are you going to choose?

I choose freedom every time and have successfully used the Quantum Sobriety approach not just on drugs and alcohol but sugar, processed foods and overeating too.

I feel that a corner has been turned with sugar and the world is waking up to its dangers, but we have an awfully long way to go to get the conditioning out of our society.

I hear the following conversations a lot at the retreat centre:

'You should let yourself have cake sometimes, on special occasions.'
'I will admit to giving sweets to my children as a treat.'
'A little of anything won't hurt.'
'You don't eat sugar? That must be awful for you!'
'I don't know how I am going to cope being here for two days without sugar.'

Firstly giving anyone anything that is causing inflammation in their bodies (see references) is most definitely not giving them a 'treat'.

Or what about:

'Have some heroin tonight, a little of anything won't hurt'

And then imagine saying this to an alcoholic:

'Go on it's a special occasion, just have one pint/glass of wine'

I think we can all agree that it would be downright out of order to say that. It is exactly the same with sugar which is now proven to be harmful and addictive (see references).

Treat or Cheat?
We have already looked closely at the language that we use in Quantum Quality Five: Quantum Jumping, and changing the word 'treat' to cheat' when talking about unhealthy foods is a very positive step. For generations we've been taught to give sweets as a 'treat', thus laying down the foundations for a future where we associate reward with sugar. Equally we are also creating a situation where we teach to 'comfort' eat when upset, which could lead to a lifetime of emotional binging.

I don't eat much fruit, other than indigenous UK fruits like apples and pears, as most fruit is high in natural sugar meaning the body still has to deal with the increase in glucose and produce more insulin; this process happens with 'good' as well as with 'bad' sugars. Now my 'treat' is a mango sorbet or raw pudding created by my talented husband, not something that I eat everyday but definitely enjoyed regularly and there's no need to go without sweet stuff altogether when using natural sweeteners.

However I literally do not ever eat any processed sugar. I read packets and turn down meals that I suspect may contain it; my body does not deserve, want or crave this poison. And just like with the drugs and alcohol there is no longing for it, no feeling of missing out when a huge birthday cake is produced or everyone else on the table at the restaurant orders pudding. I have a herbal tea instead and feel happy that I am not harming myself, which is also exactly how I feel when I now see others drinking alcohol or smoking cigarettes.

The Quantum Sobriety mind-set works for everything.

Gluten Free

Gluten is difficult for the body to break down and many people are intolerant to it. Plus the grains that we eat now are far different from those of yesteryear as we play around with the crops to make a higher yield. If you eliminate gluten from your diet your body will be under less stress, and able to use its energy on repair rather than a sluggish digestive system. Personally I eat a little gluten occasionally so that my body remembers what to do with it so that I don't create an intolerance to it.

Animal Free

I decided to become vegan for three main reasons; I am an animal lover, I found out about how much of an impact the meat/animal industry has on the environment, and intuitively for me a plant-based diet is in alignment with my highest truth and optimum health. You can do your own research on this if it resonates, and internally ask if it is the right step for you and in no way am I saying that you must take this step. It has taken me 20 years to arrive at this decision, slowly refining my diet over the last two decades.

Many wonder about calcium. Cows get calcium from grass, so as long as we are consuming our green leafy vegetables we need not worry about calcium. Drink a smoothie with veggies or have a salad or steamed veg with your dinner, and make sure you are eating a whole range of vegetables as they all contain different nutrients. The university of California says that in 1 cup of milk there is 300mg of calcium, whilst in 1 cup of cooked spinach there is 240mg.

The human body can find dairy produce difficult to digest. Although technically only having one stomach all food (grass) goes through the cow's four different compartments of this stomach, each one having a different purpose. Our bodies are not compatible with this process, and you may find that goats milk is more agreeable with your own system. There are plenty of nut milks on the market now, although it's come to light that there are only 12 almonds in a litre carton of some shop-bought brands. Make your own, it couldn't be easier:

Almond Milk Recipe
- 1 handful of nuts
- 1 pint of water
- Blend

As I said it couldn't be easier. Use more nuts for thicker milk or even 'cheese'. You will get used to the exact amount of nuts depending on your individual taste.

Processed Nightmare
Crisps, chocolate, biscuits, crackers, ready meals, sauces, ketchup, condiments, milkshakes, soft drinks, sweets, ice cream the list is endless of the complete nightmare food manufacturers have created. Could you keep a diary for a few days or week to get a picture of what processed foods you are consuming?

Each time you eat it you are becoming energetically denser and distancing yourself from your natural translucency. We want to raise ourselves up and you will find it more difficult to clear your mind in meditation if you are full of unnatural chemicals, and although more subtle, it is similar to the pendulum analogy at the beginning of this book; going from pure thought and potential to something that has been made in a factory and most probably in unhappy surroundings.

Fat Does NOT Make You Fat
We are under the incorrect spell that fat makes you fat, when it is actually sugar that is the culprit. There is now significant amounts of new scientific evidence to support this (see references), but as this whole book has shown it can be very difficult to start to think differently from the mainstream information we are fed. There is slight progress, with a few news bulletins reporting the fact and celebrity chefs talking about it, but still we get bombarded with out-dated data.

I am talking about good fats here, not highly processed trans-fats, which will play havoc with our bodies.
The brain needs good healthy fats from avocado, coconut, nuts and seeds. We should apply a good quality extra virgin olive oil to dress our vegetables but never cook with it, as it turns toxic when heated. For cooking, use coconut oil, which will withstand a very high heat.

Loved Food
When we cook food ourselves or know where it has been made we know that the intention put into the food is loving. Think about the factory production line and what the workers could be thinking,

'I hate my job. I hate my life.'
'What time is my break, I'm so bored.'
'I can't wait to get to the pub.'

Whereas when you're in a good place and feeling connected you put that connection into your cooking. Some people can even taste the difference.

Two Litres A Day
How much water do you drink daily? We need to hydrate ourselves and when we feel thirsty that means we are already dehydrated. There are so many benefits of drinking plenty of water and we must make a concerted effort to do so. Here are a few tips that work for me:
- Purchase some beautiful glass jugs or bottles and fill a few every morning and keep them around the house/office.
- Drink a pint of water at certain times of the day, even having a timer sound at each interval.
- Steep a jug of water with the following combinations:

1. Lemon
2. Lemon and ginger
3. Lemon and orange
4. Lemon, cucumber and mint
5. Mint
6. Cinnamon stick
7. Apple and cinnamon

You can get really creative with this. Just pick spices that you really love and mix and match when you feel like a change.

Hot Water and Lemon

As a drink first thing in the morning you can't get better than hot water and lemon. Make sure you put 1/3 of *cold* water in the cup first, then the lemon, and top up with hot water; otherwise you will kill the vitamin C in the lemon if you only use boiling water.

I also add a slice of fresh ginger and a capful of apple cider vinegar for a truly alkaline boost to begin my day.

The Acid / Alkaline Balance

Fast food, alcohol, fried food, stress, addiction, processed food, drugs, negativity, dairy, fizzy drinks, takeaways, etc. create an acidic environment in the body. On the other hand fresh fruits and vegetables (not all of them), water, positivity, love, happiness etc create an alkaline setting. (see references)

'NO disease, including cancer, can exist in an alkaline environment'
Dr Otto Warburg, 1931 Nobel Prize winner for cancer discovery

This couldn't be more important; we are slowing killing ourselves by eating acidic foods and having acidic thoughts and beliefs. We are in control of this, we can change it, and this book is a path to do just that. I proved this myself with my sugar experiment; the psoriasis and cyst literally didn't have anything 'feeding' them so couldn't survive. Think about what is going on inside your body, what you cannot see. Why would you knowingly harm yourself once you are armed with the knowledge that it doesn't have to be this way? This is true love and compassion to self.

Equally don't beat yourself up over this. If you've been eating a certain way your whole life it is going to take time to slowly change your habits, especially if you are also cooking for a family. It took me 20 years of gradually shifting to the reality that I am in now. Take it gently, make small changes first and remember that your 'gross' addiction, the one that you picked up this book because of is the most important change, work with that first and only begin with your food intake once you feel ready.

Fasting
As you already know I go into retreat once a year and part of this particular practice is fasting. The purpose of fasting is to develop the mind and generate compassion, gratitude and humility.
When we feel hungry the natural response is to feed ourselves, but to learn to allow the hunger to be there and get used to the feeling is very similar to overcoming the addictive urge. We can perhaps use a half-day fast every week to teach ourselves to not instantly smother our feelings as soon as they appear.

Fasting also has a very positive effect on the physical body as when we stop eating and thus digesting, the body has a chance to spend the energy it normally uses digesting food on healing and repair work.

Ultimately all of our food choices and all of the suggestions in this section are about making us feel better, giving more energy, better focus and staying young. I can say with my hand on my heart that I feel younger today than ever before.

Now who's up for some chocolate for breakfast?

Nutrition:
Chocolate For Breakfast

Chocolate 'opens' you up

There are many people out there who think they are a chocoholic when the fact is they are *not* addicted to the cacao at all; it's *sugar* they crave. Give a 'chocoholic' 100% cacao with nothing added, and they will shudder away from the bitter and mature taste, which is totally alien from what they are used to.

Chocolate Is Good For You
There is nothing wrong with eating the *right* kind of chocolate. In fact I eat it most days, and would like to share with you my chocolate journey and why I love to have it for breakfast.
The cacao that we sell at the retreat centre has been acquired for its meditation properties, with the fact that it tastes good being only an added bonus. Keith Wilson aka 'The Chocolate Shaman' sources the beans in Guatemala from the original cacao plant, which ancient Mayan shamans would have used in their ceremonies thousands of years ago. Chocolate has been used for centuries to focus the mind but was overlooked in the 1960s love revolution because it is not a psychedelic.

The Facts
Cow's milk inhibits the absorption of theobromine, the active compound in cacao. So whoever created 'milk

chocolate' was really having a laugh with us. And just a tiny fraction of the goodness remains in commercial chocolate, just a few per cent in most known brands. With the procedure that it goes through in the factory, the very high heat of the process and then the addition of milk; nothing is left other than bad fat, milk and sugar. And after the information in the last chapter about all of those things, all I can say is: Yuk, you won't catch me eating commercial chocolate.

Even the raw cacao we find in health food shops has a lower amount of active compound because most South American cacao is made from hybridised beans. Some say that cacao originated in Central America whilst others that it travelled from Ecuador or Peru north into Central America with the shamans. Perhaps only 10 per cent of the world chocolate supply comes from the smaller non-hybridized beans, and at the moment Keith is the only person in the world producing it for global shamanic ceremonial use, rather than its flavour.

Cacao Ceremonies
We came into contact with it soon after opening the retreat centre when Keith was on a world tour and looking for venues to hold 'Cacao Ceremonies', where you drink a ceremonial grade dose of chocolate as a drink, and then meditate for a few hours. We'd never heard of it, or him, but to say we were blown away by him, by the chocolate, and by the experience is an understatement. From that moment on we began to use the chocolate regularly in our retreats and classes and now hold regular Cacao Ceremonies. The chocolate 'opens' you up, connecting to the heart chakra, and enhances whatever you are doing whether that's meditation, writing, teaching, walking, sports, speaking – everything. And if

love is an elevation of self then used wisely this tool has far reaching abilities.

Cacao Ceremony
Per person

1/8 of a cup of raw ceremonial grade cacao (20g)
1/8 of a cup of cashew nuts
Add sweetener to taste (we used around 1–2 teaspoons of xylitol)
1 teaspoon of maca
1 teaspoon of lucuma
a drop of pure vanilla extract (or flavour of your choice)

Put all of your ingredients into a high-powered blender or food processor and blitz at a high speed until cashews have broken down and you are left with a smooth drink. The mixture will heat itself with friction; around 5 minutes will do it.
In a conventional blender, you may need to warm your cacao on the hob once it is a smooth consistency.
We heat ours to just below 46°C, so it is warm but still raw and not hot enough to cook out the goodies.
If you are not using cashews and water to make cashew milk you can use any nut/coconut milk. Just not animal milk, as it inhibits the uptake of the active compounds in the cacao.
Store in an airtight container/bottle in the fridge. It will last up to 3 days.

Health Benefits
You wouldn't think there were any would you? But there is a ton of them and you can watch an interview of my

husband Dom interviewing Keith and asking him just that on this link:

https://youtu.be/NUd35mSPZlg

Keith Talks About Quantum Sobriety

During a trip to Guatemala in 2015 Dom talked to Keith about the health benefits of cacao, and I interviewed him on his views about addiction.

You can watch that video here:
https://youtu.be/Nb0UcspAEj8

Counselling:
Learning To Ask For Help

Learn to ask for help

I turned up for my first counselling session with the intention of sorting out my fear of driving. Of course I didn't know it at the time but I was in fact suffering from post-traumatic stress after being in a nasty road traffic accident. I didn't drive for a number of years after it, and was a terrible passenger. I actually thought that if you arrived at your destination safely, you were lucky.

I used lack of money as the perfect excuse to not drive, but wanted to move beyond this limiting belief as I had a lovely new car on my vision board. So the sessions began talking around this subject but it soon redirected to my drinking problem (I'd given up the drugs by this time and replaced them with a nasty binge drinking habit) that I hadn't actually admitted was there. *Denial is very interesting*.

The Washing Line
There was such freedom in having an hour to talk with a complete stranger about my problems, frustrations and control issues. I could tell her *anything*, and I did. I told her things that I'd never told anyone before, and she just sat there smiling and encouraging me to open up even more. There is power in the spoken word, just like there is power in picturing your goals on paper with the vision board. Getting the words, feelings and beliefs that you've

perhaps held for a lifetime out will relieve a heaviness that you have been carrying around, so that it cannot hurt you any longer.

What it felt like to me was each subject that we spoke about was an item of clothing that I cleaned and then put on a washing line. Week after week more and more items appeared on the washing line, *to my surprise,* until I got a clear view of my whole wardrobe. I could clearly see what needed to be discarded and where the gaps for something new/more positive were. It was a truly liberating experience.

Why Taboo?

I can't believe how taboo this subject still is. How no one likes to own up to having counselling and how on TV programmes you are 'soft' if you need to talk to someone. I must own up to watching American cop/FBI/forensic type shows now and again but end up muttering under my breath or even shouting at the TV when the cop who has just been shot refuses to go to the therapist because they don't need to,

'I'm fine,' they say to their partner.

But really what is happening is they are shoving down the hurt, fear and pain so that it festers within, eventually resulting in an illness or disease. I know, I know, the show isn't real, but its millions of viewers *are* and they are getting the same message shoved down their throats that *'you are not a strong person if you talk to someone about your problems'.* It's totally back to front.

WARNING!

I had initially planned to just have four weekly sessions with my counsellor as I thought I was ok and didn't really have much 'stuff' going on, just the driving issue.

WRONG. I ended up having weekly sessions for six months and it was totally amazing. So much came up and it was during this time that I had my first bout of serious sobriety; all of a sudden because I could see so much clearer I didn't *want* to drink anymore (this hadn't happened before and was quite a shock to me). I stopped drinking for nearly six months, until Dom and I went on our honeymoon to an all-inclusive resort. I hadn't planned for or factored in the 'free' booze for two weeks and broke my sobriety with a cocktail,

'Well it's the only honeymoon I'll ever have', was the excuse I gave myself.

I drank moderately on the holiday thinking that I would easily return to sobriety on my return. WRONG. Unfortunately I drank more heavily than I had ever done before, and was engulfed in shame and disappointment.

Don't Get Cocky
The warning is of course not to get cocky like I did. It's easy to think you've got it in the bag and can 'moderately' drink just because you've been sober for a few months. Once you see alcohol for what it really is (responsible for 1 in 10 deaths in the US) then why are you hankering after being able to have it occasionally? Do you want to do the same with heroin? Or crack? This programme is about evolution to a place where none of these things are welcome, in any quantity, for they greatly *lower* our vibration.
Planning is everything. Mind-set is everything. We know this already, so when we book the all-inclusive holiday we need to *prepare* ourselves beforehand and be ready for the 'free' cocktails when they are offered.

End Date

Eventually I had all of the tools that I needed and took my last drink on 14th October 2012.

As you already know I have absolutely no desire to drink, the *charge* has gone, meaning there is no effort when I'm around drinkers to not drink myself.

My advice then is to talk to someone about what you are going through, preferably someone who has been there themselves or at the very least has the skills to support you.

You may choose counselling, psychotherapy, coaching or a residential programme. Shop around, have a taster session to see if you have a connection to the therapist and feel that you can open up to them. But please do not try to do this by yourself, learn to ask for help, and as soon as you do the quantum will busily organise the ideal person to support your journey.

Journalling:
Writing It All Down

By writing it down, just like when we talk to someone,
we are getting the problem out of ourselves

The last helper in this section is something that I have done for as long as I can remember: write a journal, or diary. I began decades ago longhand and now find it quicker and more efficient on a small laptop. Find what works for you and begin chronicling your journey. Sometimes the changes that we make are so imperceptible that we don't realise that they are happening, and then we can read back on our journal and see in black and white exactly how far we've come.

The other important reason is that by writing it down, just like when we talk to someone, we are getting the problem *out* of ourselves. Sometimes it's like we are having a conversation with our self. Many times I have begun writing feeling one way and then answered my own question by the time I've got halfway down the page. You will gain clarity and a feeling of great relief. It's a little like doing the Trigger Meditation from Quantum Quality Two where you get your addiction onto the table in front of you and have a look at it in great detail; you see it differently from another perspective, like seeing with another's eyes.

I write early and doing this every day gets me clear about where I'm at and where I need to put my attention during the course of the day. Combined with meditation as part of a morning routine, these two activities will get you exactly where you need to be to have the highest vibe start to your day.

Buy a new book and pen or create a new folder on your computer, and start to log your progress on this path.

Non-Negotiables

This section forms what I call my non-negotiables; things that keep me on track and focused on staying connected and moving forwards. For years I have tried to work out the winning formula, and we each have one, and the trick is to keep changing it until you hit the bull's-eye. The following is my own personal morning routine but please chop and change the activities and times to suit your own personality.

6am Alarm
6:30am Journalling and blogging
8:30am Meditation
9:30am Breakfast, juice or smoothie
10am The day begins

This may change slightly when I am away but I have formulated this so that no matter what usually goes on in my life, it can work around these timings.

Everything on this list raises my vibration and makes me feel more alive, and it has become so easy to get up early so I have time for each activity so that my day begins in the best possible way.

First thing in the morning when I am still connected deeply to the subconscious mind is when I like to write and meditate. This is when the veil of conditioning is lifted, and for me offers a magical time of being able to channel what I am feeling onto the page. Sometimes I meditate first and then write, other times the other way around, but these two activities form the infrastructure of everything else in my day.

You have to work out what is right for you, and most people do not have the luxury of the extended time I have to do this. But make no mistake I have created my life exactly how I want it; carved out a routine that suits me personally, and the rest of my day sits around this foundation.

I also have an afternoon and evening routine, and this is where some sort of daily exercise sits along with night time meditation.

We are each different, with unique responsibilities and commitments. Maybe right now you can only commit to 10 minutes meditation and 10 to write each morning, and that is totally fine. But watch as the opportunity to expand that presents itself to you, if that is your intention, for the quantum will always provide what you ask for.

Epilogue:
The Journey From Head To Heart

It's like putting on rose-tinted glasses that you never have to take off

All of the meditations, exercises and guidance have been leading you to the heart, which is electromagnetically far more powerful than the brain. This is where again science and spirituality join together and we can *prove* that what we are feeling on the inside mirrors our outer landscape.

The heart is intelligent and around 60 times stronger electrically than the brain (see references). So can you see how powerful all of the exercises and meditations in this book are? That if you maintain neutrality, the zero point, the quantum field, the peace that meditation brings, coherence, whatever you want to call it, you are plugging in to your heart. This is spirituality backed up with science.

As soon as you connect with an awareness of who you are; forgiveness, compassion, love, acceptance, belief in your power, gratitude and trust, you immediately connect with the heart and are thus living from it. You know instinctively whether you are doing this or not: if you feel irritated, angry, triggered to eat/drink/drug, depressed or stressed, you are in your head and it's time to come back to stage one, Awareness, and bring yourself back down into connected heart energy. You could say your Quantum

Superpower is actually LOVE with meditation fast-tracking the connection.

Maintenance Of The Practice
All of the way through this book you have been learning how to meditate and I do hope you have now secured a daily practice. Ideally you have found a local teacher to connect in person with and meditate in a group setting. Couple that with daily recordings (mine or another's) and you will have all you need to stabilise your practice.

Each 'sitting' we are mind training; creating new pathways and possibilities. On some days this will be easy and we 'get' it whilst on others the 'space' we are searching for seems fleeting. The quality of the practice does not matter, the *only* thing that matters is actually doing the meditation because every single time you sit on your cushion you are sending a message to the brain and something is happening, even if we don't notice it.

Collapsing Time
When we begin to live this we understand that whatever we programme our minds to believe, we'll manifest and witness in our day-to-day reality. If we can do 'An Alternate Reality' meditation so much that when we step onto the quantum field and into our highest potential it becomes our new normal, then we just began to live ahead of time. Because we are choosing that experience and the quantum *has to* give it to you. There can be no argument, no mistake; your external environment has to catch up with your mind. You hear that? You understand that fully? For it's the law!
As we've seen in the Quantum Jumping chapter our concept of time is challenged, and we begin to understand that by collapsing time we can have anything because it already exits. However, we can only experience

what we believe and consequently choose.

Really linear time does not exist; 'time' is something that humans have created to make sense of something we do not understand. Scientists tell us (see references) there is no reason the past, present and future cannot be accessed in the exact same way; we just cannot comprehend that, *yet*.

The Magic Button

Something that has helped me greatly is lightly placing my index finger and thumb together in stressful situations or when I am not feeling connected to my Quantum Superpower. Because we sit like this daily during our meditation, as soon as we do this when we are tense our mind automatically goes back to the calm state of meditation. It is ideal when stuck in a traffic jam, the post office queue or around highly stressed people.

I also sometimes use this technique when I'm eating a meal as it's easy to get caught up in conversation or watching TV and not be very mindful of what you are doing. Connecting back to your essence and enjoying the process of ingestion means you enjoy your dinner all the more. In fact wherever I am and whatever I'm doing, if I need to get connected quickly this is often the easiest way to do so.

When I taught yoga and meditation to children in schools we called this our 'magic button'. The children soon realised that no one needed to know that they were pressing their magic buttons under the table or with their hands in their pockets; they immediately had a way out of a stressful situation, and a doorway into their inner world.

Buddha In The City

It is wonderful being in retreat, whether that is during our daily meditation or in a class, but the real challenge of course is to bring a Buddha quality into your normal life. This is actually the whole point of meditation; this is what it does for us, how it changes us. As already discussed we have our 'formal' training sitting on our cushion and the rest of our lives is our 'informal' practice.

I know when I go on retreat myself that I have managed to maintain the magic for up to three months on returning home. That time however was always cut off *immediately* when I started drinking; sometimes on the train coming home from the retreat. And how annoyed with myself I would be. What a waste of a feeling of peace. Instantly ruined by alcohol, which literally stole the magical feeling from me.

Bullets Of Peace

We take the SPACE we have created in our practice and carry it with us like we have an extended presence. Can you imagine that you have an invisible shield around you extending ten inches in all directions? It is protecting you from all outside influences: sounds, energy and stress. Have you seen on TV the crime scene programmes where they shoot a bullet into a tank of jelly, which slows the bullet down until it is stationary? Well that is what your invisible shield is doing. When you connect to your true self in meditation you build up this invisible shield so that outside stimuli slows down as it comes towards you. Rather than life being in your face with no protection from it at all, you get warning, you have PERSPECTIVE so that rather than *react* immediately without any thought you have time to *respond* as you wish to; for your highest good.

This is how you use your Quantum Superpower

This is how you transform your life. Can you see how important it is to keep topping up your power (with meditation) so that it doesn't wear off? Do you get it? It's amazing isn't it!

If you don't meditate everyday and keep building up your shield you start losing your power. When you have had an intense period of practice like a retreat, then you are running at full power and must do everything in your control to maintain it if you are to experience life with continued wonder.

You CHOOSE what comes into your energy field. *You* have a choice of what comes in. And when you are vibrating at this higher level, the maximum that you are able to at that given time, then it becomes easy to do this. Life becomes an enchanted game as you watch the ripples of stress come towards you but now you know how to deal with them, that they hurt you only if you allow them to; that you have a choice.

It is revolutionary for most of us to realise that this is possible, and it will transform your life in so many beautiful ways. It's like putting on rose-tinted glasses that you never have to take off. This is the power, your superpower, with the quantum all around listening to every single thought, word and action that comes into our consciousness; a loving intelligence that will respond to your intentions by giving you the best it possibly can. And what you receive is so often not what you expect it is going to be (it's usually better), and this is a huge stumbling block for us to relinquish control and allow what we never thought possible to happen. There is quite literally magic wherever you look, but most of the time we are too busy or too stressed to notice. Can you *slow down* and see it?

Be The Change

Gandhi's quote has never made more sense than in the context of neuroplasticity, and it is here that the 'old' and 'new' worlds collide so beautifully.

'Be the change you want to see in the world'

As I've been writing this book I keep getting flashbacks to the 'old' Jo, almost like I am in the same room comforting this sad, confused and stressed individual. In fact this is who I have written the book for because I know there are so many people out there who *want* a happier life, *know* on a DNA level that it's possible, but don't know *how* to achieve it.

Quantum Grow Bag

You have all of the information now, and it's time to create a new enhanced life. Just like someone would have plastic surgery to fix what he or she was unhappy about on the outside, we do the same from the inside outwards. We either live from the primal part of our brain, the amygdala, connected to the fight or flight response and always guaranteed to cause us stress and keep us in the past; or we catapult ourselves into the future, turning on the frontal lobe: home to creativity, intentions, happiness and peace.

We get connected to our truth and our heart in meditation; step out onto the quantum field and in doing so create a force field around ourselves, and this is the fertile ground of the quantum grow bag; seeds can now be planted here and as long as you stay connected they grow and flourish.

So here you are sitting inside your grow bag, your energy field fully expanded (it can get to around 9 metres wide) and you then physically *grow into* the future that you've already mapped out in your head and on your vision board; you know where you are going; the scene is set; you've just got to stay connected to your Quantum Superpower, believe, and step into that parallel universe.

Watch your whole life transform. Better relationships, content outlook, the best of health, a job that you love, heart overflowing and living your life *on purpose*. You have picked up this book or it has somehow found its way to you (like quantum glue), *it is mirroring you*, plus you've made it through to the end. What this means is that you are ready, right now, for transformation.

The Journey From Head To Heart
We get out of our heads and into our hearts by developing our ability to 'turn on' gratitude, love, forgiveness, acceptance, belief and trust. The 'Reflections' all the way through this book have been exercises in doing just that, in finding the connection, sustaining it, and then living it. The activity and therefore balance between the different areas of the brain shifts, and we find we are less angry, less worried, and have fewer problems in our life. All of this because we learnt to develop the higher emotions of the heart, with meditation being our express train to connection. We will know when we're off course, because the fear and lack will rise once more. So we go back down to the heart, listen to our truth and find peace once more.

A Beacon Of Authentic Truth
When we learn to turn inwards and connect with our inner dialogue (rather than be carried off on external frequencies), and work through each of the eight Quantum Qualities (and their helpers), we then light up our Inner Guidance System and we ourselves become

beacons of authentic truth. Just like a lighthouse we send out a signal with every beat of our heart, and in this way, once all connected, we become a sea of heightened consciousness spreading out to all corners of the globe.

This is the next generation of sobriety, and you are part of this revolution towards freedom.
Welcome to Quantum Sobriety...

Quantum Sobriety

Index Of Meditations And Exercises

Meditations

Exercises

Testimonial From The Expert

Lucy Rocca,
Founder of Soberistas

'Quantum Sobriety' is a brilliantly accessible and encouraging read, perfect for anyone wanting to escape the confines of addiction but who doesn't know where to start. Mindfulness together with an awareness of how the brain works with regards to addiction have been fantastically helpful in my own battle with alcohol dependency, and the easy-to-understand way in which Jo explains these concepts in Quantum Sobriety is sure to help anyone looking for a practical guide with which to beat their addiction/s. Successfully conquering her own persistent demons along with the years she spent studying Buddhist meditation techniques with inspirational teachers have combined to give Jo the knowledge and experience that this book is built on. You can't inspire anyone to get sober unless you have been there and done it yourself and Jo's candid account of her own years lived on a self-destructive mission is something I could totally relate to. This very readable book is a no-nonsense guide to sorting out your life and headspace in a non-preachy and completely down to earth manner.

Testimonials From The QS Community

The first eight testimonials are from the Quantum Guides; members who have been through the programme themselves and are out the other side into freedom. The Quantum Guides form part of Jo's team, supporting her and the community at large. As QS grows there is an increasing need for the Guides to reply to the numerous comments and questions on the forum. They all have *at least* nine months of sobriety.

Sophie, UK

QS, quite simply, changed my life. I found out about the venue (not the programme) from a friend. On googling it, I read about Jo and the 5-day addiction retreats she ran. It was a possibility for sorting out my alcohol problem (I had tried several times to give up over the years, including a brief foray into AA). I was a functioning alcoholic. I'd never missed a day of work because of it. However, all I did for the most part was work and drink and I could feel myself tipping over the edge. I'd had enough. The retreat was expensive, however, and I couldn't afford it. I'm also quite analytical, was a bit cynical, and I was not sure it was my 'thing'. I filed it away in the back of my mind.

About a year later I had a rare two weeks' holiday from work (the first 'two weeker' in many years). One week was accounted for but I wasn't sure what to do with the other. Amazingly (or so I thought at the time) there was a QS 5-day residential retreat on. I phoned up Jo and went for it. I joined the online programme in the June and booked on to the 5-day retreat in August. I received the first meditation audio and got stuck in. Every day I sat on my mat doing the Trigger meditation, every day I 'went to the conference room', and every day no one came. I had no helpers, no guides, no higher beings, nothing. The second month I received the Alternate Reality meditation. I moved onto this one. I 'went to the archway' through which my alternate reality apparently resided. Nothing. It was completely blank. I doggedly carried on with my meditation practice every day. Reminding myself of Jo's words – keep an open mind.

The online forum associated with the programme was an amazing bunch of people all at different stages in their addiction journeys. Some had been alcohol free for months. How was this even possible? Incredible. I observed it all. People were open about their struggles, their successes, their triggers and others were supporting them, no judgement. It felt like a safe place. I was no longer alone with my addiction. Jo was everywhere. She was online daily with her morning blogs, responding to posts, running an interactive livestream each week, an interactive webinar once a month. The support was incredible. Yet I confess I was still struggling to give up alcohol.

The retreat came around and I arrived full of apprehension (how could five days make a difference) but along I went with my slippers and an open mind. The first couple of days of the retreat changed my life forever. I examined and started to let go of the past, forgave myself, took responsibility and moved on. My meditations changed too (I had a helper in my conference room; there was something through the archway). I was beginning to understand how the quantum worked and how my thoughts and actions changed things around me. Five days later, I was equipped and ready to get on with my life.

I stayed close to the group, visited the online forum every day, participated in the livestreams and webinars and, because I could, I paid regular visits to the centre for meditation practice and had therapy sessions with the amazing Carol and Anni.

Nearly a year on (I write this in 2017), my meditation practice (the cornerstone of my sobriety) gets stronger every day and I am embracing life and the opportunities it offers. I see that everything is connected and that everything happens for a reason. My life is completely different now (in fact big changes occurred for me within 5 months). In practical terms, I very quickly 'came out' about my hidden 35-year problem with alcohol, I changed my job of 25 years, a couple of other major things, and I found my life. Oh and I no longer drink (almost forgot that). It's brilliant!

I'll be a part of the QS programme and community for as long as Jo will have me and was both honoured and humbled when she asked me to be a QS Guide. Every single person on the programme is an important and integral part of the whole. I want to shout about QS from the rooftops. Everyone should have the opportunity to find their life and to enjoy the freedom and happiness that I do now.

Right at the beginning I asked myself – can I afford to do this? I ask you now, can you afford not to?

Nikki, USA
QS: Powerfull Not Powerless

I called for help in my absolute drunkenness. I called a rehab facility having been on my first and only 10,11,12, or 13 day binge of alcohol and Zanax. I still don't know how long it was. You know the blackout routine.

I remember pouring a beer into my coffee mug on the way to the hospital out of fear of falling completely apart while my 80 year old father guided me down the steps to the car. Remembering this now, hurts. But, I take a breath and know that the hurt needed to happen. All of it. For now I am liberated from all that ugly, all that deception.

As I began my sober self study before Quantum Sobriety it rattled me to no end as to how I became unable to control my drinking and drugging. I wanted to point my finger at some event or situation that caused my inability to control it all. Like many, I wanted an explanation. HOW did I get here? WHY did I get here? I was newly sober going through rehab in and out patient. I was sad. I was full of shame and guilt. I was blindsided by my own choices and self-destruction.

AA was imbedded in my rehab program as it is in most hospitals here in the United States. I can vividly remember the very first time I asserted "I'm Nicole, and I'm an alcoholic." Ironically, I've never felt so "powerless." Sure, I saw the sad, sick, and self-destructive self, but I NEVER EVER felt that THAT was going to be how I defined myself for the rest of my life...an alcoholic. Just in THAT alone, I knew AA was not a fit for me. Don't get me wrong...I don't want to forget what alcohol created in me; I believe that is a powerful teacher. But, with QS, practice, and my guiding angels, I have created "a life as if I've never been addicted."

I found Jo's lecture about her initial launch of the online QS program ONE WEEK before she launched it. (Jo could probably search her records for the actual date I signed up.) I googled "Alternatives to AA" and I was directed to the Soberista's website. When Jo was telling HER STORY, I felt as if it could be mine. Snorting cocaine up my nose and gulping copious amounts of booze to wake up and do a yoga class in a foreign country. Cleopatra meets Eat Pray Love style. I saw her and saw myself. I saw her and said, "That's me. I am that. I will be that. Where is her bus stop?" Without any hesitation, I signed up.

My interest in quantum physics probably began with the documentary "What the Bleep Do We Know" whenever it first came out. After watching that, I read as much as I could about the Water Experiment and started paying attention to my intentions, my worries, my fears.

Fast forward to the QS launch... I thought, "Wow, this woman is taking sobriety and addiction and applying the laws of quantum physics with dedicated meditations/teachings while fostering a community of like-minded individuals???" B R I L L I A N T. The concept of rewiring your "plastic" brain made complete sense to me. Jo's concept was in complete alignment with my desired path. We are powerful. We can control what we put in our bodies.

I had already experienced this technology with the practice of kundalini yoga in my 20s when I experienced intense panic attacks of uncontrollable vomiting when confronted with stress or excitement. With the kundalini practice, I was able to change my nervous system's reaction to stress and excitement.

I understood and BELIEVED in our ability to change our reality.

Experiencing this positive change, I was reminded of the Water Experiment that resonated so deeply with me and gave me proof that our intentions can and do create reality. As I found myself in another vulnerable place in life trying to stay sober, all of this came back to me when I found QS.

QS gave me a community at the time of my critical sober 'birthing year'. QS gave me guided meditations to nurture my recovery. The meditations helped me forgive, let go, call upon the universe for assistance, see that "I am enough", look at my relationship with food and caffeine, and has provided me with many profound realization visualizations. I don't always get on my cushion. But, my intention is there.

 Now, I hold my head high. Now, I have tough conversations instead of avoiding them. Now, I more gently accept that not everyone is going to understand me. Now, I have people in my life who live from their hearts. Now, I maneuver through conflict and stress with more grace. Now, I have mindful moments daily. Now, I have more compassion for myself and others. All of what I have NOW is my answer. The answer to HOW and WHY I found sobriety and Quantum Sobriety.

After experiencing what Jo calls the birthing and first year of sobriety, Jo asked me to be a guide. Without hesitation again and with the roles of the guides unfolding before us, I am honored, happy, and proud to represent the NEXT MOVEMENT OF TRUE SOBRIETY, BEAUTY, AND FREEDOM. I believe in Jo and QS so much so that even from waaaay across the Big Blue sea, it's a part of my new life. Though I may not be as active on the forum or I may comment on a post at 2am UK time, know that it's just a flicker of light from Los Angeles reaching across the

Quantum. I hope to see QS explode all over the world and look forward to QS coming to a city near me soon. This is a program for the consciousness of today.

....

Hazel, Scotland
Having realised that I didn't have much of an off button when it came to alcohol, and completely fed up of wasting so much time recovering from the after-effects, I realised that the best option for me was to stop drinking altogether. By the end of January 2016 I had been alcohol-free for 8 months, but at a personal level I certainly didn't feel free. Stopping drinking had thrown up all sorts of unexpected emotions and questions, along with the realisation that I had been using alcohol as a crutch in many ways. The self-confidence I thought I'd had, had evaporated and I knew I needed some tools to work through all of this. Although my life was so much better after ditching alcohol, I still felt like I was missing out, and I knew if this carried on I'd never stick with it. Just 2 days after QS launched, I happened to come across it via Jo's Webinar on Soberistas and signed up to the online programme. Meditation in general, and the tailored QS meditations have given me invaluable tools to change the way that I feel and think. Alcohol had for so many years been my main tool to change my state, but in meditation I found something far deeper and far more effective. In the period since I've been part of QS I have had my wedding, honeymoon, 25 year college reunion, along with some stressful situations to deal with. QS has been invaluable in maintaining my sobriety throughout all of these potentially challenging situations through the accountability and new mindset that it brings, along with the support from Jo and the amazing wider QS community. I am delighted to be a QS Guide and to now be able to start paying it forward.

Theresa, UK

I first met Jo several years ago when I attended her meditation and gong wash class at her house in Ware, Hertfordshire. Jo told me she was moving and opening up an retreat centre in Suffolk, I followed her big move to Inner Guidance on facebook and via her announcements about what was happening. I attended a few retreats at the retreat centre and felt such an amazing connection to the house and to Jo's dream.

I had struggled for several years with overeating and a sugar addiction, this was all brought on by bullying I suffered as an early teenager. I never told anyone about the bullying till I was in my late 30's and used food and sugar as an emotional support, I hated myself and my confidence was low.

I was receiving regular newsletters from Jo and one day something grabbed my eye, a new programme that Jo was launching called 'Quantum Sobriety' now automatically I was like this is for drugs and alcohol not for my issues with food and sugar. I rang and spoke to Jo and she said it would be great for me. I decided to take the plunge, I needed to change my relationship with food and to stop letting it rule my life.

I joined the online programme in February 2016 with my eyes wide open to new possibilities and a new life ahead. I loved getting the email from Jo every month with the new meditation, I experienced so many emotions during these meditations, happy and sad tears but these spurred me to keep going, I could see some amazing changes happening in me.

Supporting the programme is the online Facebook community, or as I like to call them my 'quantum family', we have all become so close, being able to reach out when you are feeling triggered or even just to encourage each other with positive images, words or videos. Just knowing that someone was there was huge for me.

It is now May 2017 and what can I say, I am now 14 months sugar free and feeling totally amazing, I truly love myself and I am soaring. Food is now not used to comfort but to fuel me and I like to fuel my body with amazing food not junk and sugar. Something big happened in October 2017 my dad passed away, it was a huge shock, and without having this amazing programme and support from the online community, I would have ended up back to square one with food being my best friend and not just something that I need for fuel. Meditation is a huge part of my life now and I feel truly blessed to have found this programme.

It doesn't matter what your addiction is, alcohol, drugs, food, sugar, this programme is revolutionary and it has simply changed my life. I feel totally honoured to now be a Quantum Guide with the programme and I cannot wait to see where my life will go now.

Richard, UK

" "You are no longer scary"
These are the words spoken to me from my brother Adrian.

Adrian passed November 20th 2016.

On the 31st October 2015, my life had become so out of control, that Sunday morning I took a overdose of medication. The next morning after leaving the hospital I checked myself into Inner Guidance Retreat Centre. Since then I have been able to turn my life around. Gone are the addictions to alcohol drugs and medication (SSRIs). My relationship with my family is now full of love and compassion.

Adrian's last year alive I spent some very special moments and days with him, just like when we were kids.
This would not have been possible if I was using alcohol and drugs.

With the love and support of Jo De Rosa and all the team at QS , also the support of the online forum you too can achieve a life of Freedom.

Peace Love and Strength
Richard"

Dara, Ireland
"I've always wanted more, since I was a child. More cake, more books, more playtime. As a teenager, I wanted more music, more discos, more kisses, more phone conversations with friends ten minutes after arriving home from school. When I started drinking alcohol as a young adult, 'more' gradually became 'never enough'. I didn't know it, but what was 'not enough' was my perception of myself. I remember aged 12 trying to act like one friend because everyone liked her. Later, I tried so hard to be 'one of the lads', it became a badge of honour to be able to drink anyone under the table. I had to prove myself. Alcohol took me out of my self-doubt and into a place where I could connect with people, where I could feel 'as good as' anyone else. But it also made me a toxic person, an unstable person, an underachiever, an unpredictable mother. After many years, and several attempts to cut back or quit, alcohol made me hate myself. When I finally realised that I had an addiction and I needed help to release it, I found Quantum Sobriety.

Suddenly, it all became so simple. Choose your reality. Decide not be addicted anymore and live your life from that reality. Meditate. Learn tools that put the power back in your hands. Choose self-love over self-abuse. That's what QS teaches, ultimately. The only cure for addiction is self-love. It's a gradual process, but after doing the first meditation, I was instantly free of any desire to drink. It was that powerful. From that day – 12 April 2016 – my focus has been on how to love myself. How to remember that I AM ENOUGH. I always was. I have been learning how to come back to the 12 year old girl, dancing at the local disco, feeling so free and so… herself. Complete, happy, fully in the moment and not needing anything more. This feeling of being enough and being happy in the moment is what allows me to expand my life in any direction I choose, a joyful freedom that I didn't think possible before I joined QS."

Victoria, UK
"Drinking doesn't get in the way of Yoga.

Well it doesn't. I drank for years and years. My relationship with alcohol has been every bit as sporadic as any other relationship. It started with the odd fling. Until it became this habitual comfortable routine of just semi oblivion. There were some very dark times when it was a full on obsessive needy co-dependency. Real Cathy and Heathcliff stuff.

I was never a full on cliché of an alcoholic, slurping down vodka for breakfast. In 41 years of life I had only ever woken up once with a stranger which is pretty good going. Alcohol has only made me vomit on 3 occasions in this life. Granted I do have a fairly robust constitution. I rarely drank so much that I could not get up and work the next day, go to the gym. And Yes… Oh Yes… I am a Yogi. Who also happens to teach Yoga.

In the Yoga World there is a lot of judgement around drinking. A lot of people who say things like "Well I've never understood drinking. I mean life is so beautiful, why would you not want to be present?" Or they helpfully point out that alcohol is a toxin. As if we all didn't know

I on the other hand completely understand why people want to drink. This beautiful and infuriating world we live in seems to be Hell-bent on destroying itself. And the expectations that are placed on us and those we place on ourselves. Who wouldn't want respite?

When I was 30 I fell in love with my best friend. I met him just after the death of my father and he was really everything to me. I was living down in Brighton and we were out all the time. For the first time in my life I was in a healthy relationship with a man who didn't make me feel small, or invisible, but beautiful and cherished and important. Who got excited about my dreams and loved what I loved. Then one day, after two years, we went for a walk to the beach and he was quiet as I chattered away about plans I had, and what I had bought for when we moved in together. He suddenly stopped me. And said "I don't think I want this". And at that moment something inside me shattered. Six weeks followed of him being distant but not ending it. No, that work was left up to me but he couldn't hide his relief when I did. Even kissed me for the first time in weeks.

I spent the next few months drinking heavily. 2 bottles of wine or so a night. I was so angry and heartbroken and bereaved. Full of this insane energy as if something had taken me over. Then one day when I was totally out of it at work it occurred to me I could just leave. I had money in the bank I had been saving for a house deposit for us. So I took off to India for a few months instead. And swapped my wine addiction for Ashtanga Yoga asana addiction. Big huge dramatic detox. It didn't help as much as I thought it would. I got home and although the initial grief had worn off I could not stand to be with myself so kept on drinking.

Then the drinking wound down and got less dramatic but 9 years later it was still there. Life had changed, I was no longer working in a shop but had got better work plus building my own business as a Yoga teacher was going well.

But the state of my own inner world still meant I craved Space. I was overworked for a long time. Holding down an office job to pay the bills. Teaching most days. Rarely days off. Managing my practice maybe 3 times a week Feeling guilty and tired. I was drinking 2-3 glasses of wine 2-3 times a week. 2-3 bottles a week, not enough for anyone to be calling AA but more than enough to affect my energy levels. Always home late and alone after teaching and being on buses as I had no car. I had made the decision to keep my Yoga teaching in gyms, in schools, to my local University Yoga society. In the community. So there was a lot of rushing about. I was busier and busier, lonelier and lonelier.

So I decided to stop drinking. Just stop completely. Not 'moderate' as that doesn't work. I found online support and I found QS. Summer was coming. The first month was hard. Cravings. I would get this intense feeling of wanting to be 'elsewhere' and interpret that as boredom. I needed to sleep a lot. The sugar cravings were insane.

I started with the Trigger meditation and started to examine what was really going on. And this has been an ongoing, sometimes really painful, and sometimes an ecstatic process. The support of the QS facebook forum has been invaluable.

As I had been drinking for years all the things I used to have a drink to take the edge off came up again. My father's death. The pain of being left by the conscious choice of suicide. The death of all the people I have loved. Living alone and missing companionship. Anger. Being totally fucking furious at the man I had loved with all my heart who had left me, as it turned out, for someone else. And then, unexpectedly, thinking of him with Love. And remembering the good times.

The Quantum Sobriety support group with Jo De Rosa who I call 'The High Priestess of Sobriety' is AMAZING. This is a non judgemental approach to recovering from the habits that no longer serve you. The emphasis is on meditation and going within. There is no helpless victim thinking. I saw how my fondness for alcohol was actually a blessing. It was signposting that which I needed to attend to. So in this way addiction is a good thing. Cravings are a good thing on a soul level.

I have started to deal with the past. And to deal with the anger. And to have compassion rather than judgment. To notice my own projections and triggers. Particularly in the whole 'Yoga World' thing. My body dysmorphia and disordered eating habits are also starting to change. Accepting myself just as I am is a work in process.

My beliefs about alcohol have changed forever. I used to buy into the myth of it being relaxing. But it really is not. Ethanol has addictive qualities and we are all vulnerable. Alcohol is also marketed to be very appealing. If I was of a mindset that did conspiracy theories I would say that alcohol is the ultimate tool of social control. It is a depressant- so keeps us small. You don't even need huge mounts it for it to take the edge off your vision. It encourages you to accept the drudgery of daily life and crave escape from that rather that to CHANGE your own reality so you have a life you don't want to drink your way out of. It makes you crave shit food and keeps you sick. It makes you fat. It supports the pharmaceutical and the diet industries. Physically and emotionally it enslaves you.

Quitting drinking forever has been one of the most liberating things i have ever done. And best of all. It was easy. It's like being a child again. You wake up fresh. I swear the world looks more beautiful. I see beauty in the little things now and see the world in all its nuances. Yes I still get angry and want change but I FEEL things rather than just reacting to them. I FEEL myself rather than just reacting to others.

I have always meditated but my practice has deepened immeasurably. In Yoga it now feels as though I am there one hundred percent. I keep getting more work doing what I love. I even passed my driving test and got a car which I thought would NEVER happen.
Sobriety has now become an intrinsic part of who I am. I have changed my mind about drinking. For me, it had its place. It was useful. Sometimes I loved it. But I have loved stepping away from it.. For in quitting a habit, in letting go of a crutch you come closer to your own core. There is a rawness to it. Authentic as a child.

Drinking does NOT get in the way of Yoga. But given time, Yoga gets in the way of drinking.

I no longer see alcohol as a source of pleasure. My pleasure comes from other sources.

I have been free of alcohol for a year now. And there is a big difference between freedom and self denial. All I am denying myself now is self loathing and sickness. I was so ready to stop hating myself. And I feel I have reclaimed my power. I stand my ground now in a way I could not a year ago. And there are new opportunities in relationships presenting themselves. A massive shift from feeling unlovable. Alcohol just fertilises negativity.

Meditation and Quantum Sobriety has helped me to see all this and my life has changed forever. I will not go back to drinking. I could never go back to drinking knowing what I know now. When the odd thought of drinking comes up it is so easy to turn it around. I never ever thought that would happen. I am so grateful."

Jayne, UK
"I had been a weekend binge drinker for many years and someone who loved to party, it was part of my lifestyle and I presumed I would grow out of it, but that didn't happen.
I had been working in the Fitness Industry for years and I coped ok with the drinking as I was so fit and I didn't feel guilty about it, but as time went on I did wonder how old I would be when I finally calmed down.

As I moved more into the Mind, body and coaching field, my drinking did start to bother me more. I started to feel a bit like a fraud and guilty that people were paying me to help them with their stress and deeper challenges.

I used to have a voice that constantly said things like "Do you think you would be better at this if you hadn't drank so much at the weekend"… "Are you good enough to do this, when you drink so much?"…. "Do you think you are giving them your best?" .. "Who are you to help someone else, when you can't even moderate your own drinking?... You get used to living with this as it's subtle but it does take an effect on your self belief and self esteem over time and at some point something is going to tip and it did.

I reached my enough point after a drunken tantrum at home after a good night out. This was not usual for me, I was usually a happy, fun loving drunk person, a bit loud and silly and at the worst a drunken argument very occasionally with a loved one, but this time was different. I had been dealing with some life stress and I had stopped enjoying drinking. I noticed I felt numb or worse every time I drank, it wasn't fun and I drank for fun.

This particular night for the first time I lost control. My tantrum came out of nowhere and I did not feel it coming and nothing happened to set it off. This was my enough point.

I had scared myself and realised that I had to get really clear headed to deal with the underlying stress of what was going on. I knew though that if I went a week or two without drinking I would think I had done well and it was ok to drink, only it wasn't ok anymore as how did I know that I would not get upset and shout my stress out again, with no control.

I also knew that all it would take was a special event for me to tell myself it was ok to drink , but even this felt wrong now.

I knew this would happen as I had done this time and time again, telling myself I would have a break , cut down, stop, but It never lasted.

I couldn't trust myself, so I made a decision and called JO.

I already knew Jo from social media and I had been down to the retreat center before, so I was well aware of what she was about and I knew how worked and what she was about really resonated with me, so I joined the program and that was it.

The relief when I joined the program was so big, it was shocking. I really understood in that moment how much my drinking had been bothering me.

I got into the program straight away and it really resonated with me. To be honest it was an easy fit as I already meditated and had trained as a teacher in meditation, only I used to use it to balance out the drinking.

I understood all Jo's teaching and where she was coming from and I knew what she spoke was the truth.
The other people in the group are fantastic and the support is just invaluable and makes such a difference. Some of the people I have met in the group will probably be friends for life, because we have shared a profound and intimate journey into change and change is what this program gives you.

It's not about the drinking or the drugs.. It's about healing whatever lies beneath that, so you are free.

I would without a doubt recommend this program to anyone who is struggling with addiction and wants to really get free of it, not just stop the behaviour for it is very possible through this program.

Over a year in, I am the person I was meant to be. The peace of not having that voice anymore is life changing itself. You just don't realise how much it drags you down, till you don't have it. That is a massive freedom in itself and to grow from there takes you further than you ever thought possible, which is what this program supports."

The QS Community At Large

Kirsty, Scotland
"Quantum Sobriety has completely changed my life, in so many beautiful ways. When I joined in April 2016, I was desperate. My 20 year history of heavy drinking had slowly been ramping up 10 gears and was building into a horrid crescendo. I was either drinking 2 bottles of wine or practically a bottle of gin, almost daily. I was binge eating, preferred to drink on my own and wasn't looking after myself or my home. In March 2016 I was violent to a family member (this is so unlike me, not a violent bone in my body) and knew I needed to find help. I had tried AA 5 years previous but felt so out of place. I was petrified of some of the folk in the meeting and felt no kin-ship there. The AA story certainly didn't resonate with my soul and the content seemed so damning and heavy.

I remember asking the Universe for help. To find me something that would help me stop drinking and address my issues but with a spiritual twist that resonated with me. This was the end of March 2016. By the 4th April, I had found QS on the Soberistas website and had signed up for the online programme. 'Learn how to create a reality as if you'd never been addicted' Jo puts forward. Challenge on I thought. I was in a constant battle of waking up feeling horrendous, negative self hate chat all day, the never agains, eat crap food and by 5pm, I had convinced myself that buying 2 bottles of wine, just one more night, would be the answer.

For Jo to say I could feel like I was never addicted sounded amazing and I was very keen to try QS. Is this Jo De Rosa a magician? Well yes, as it turns out, she is! I was invited to join the secret Facebook community and did my daily meditations religiously. It was amazing to feel part of a group that understood me. To be part of a community of like-minded, loving, supportive souls that were all going through similar stuff. Doing the meditations and checking in daily with the group became my new addiction. I cannot begin to thank the on-line community enough for their love and support over the last year. An amazing bunch of people. Fact.
Each new month, I looked forward to the new meditation. My connection to source was growing strong and I felt a deep connection with myself. I was finally starting to heal. Meditation, without a doubt, has completely rewired my brain. I am sober, no more negative chat, I am happy and I love myself. QS provides the amazing tools to develop this. I have had some epic meditations and now do daily rituals that nourish my soul. Not rob myself of self esteem and self respect. I am a completely different person now and will be eternally grateful to Jo, the team behind QS and all the gorgeous folks in the QS community.

Now just to add, I have had relapses but that is no reflection on Jo's work or Quantum Sobriety. Doing the meditations daily is paramount. Taking the time to do this and develop self care is a must. The ebbs and flows of life happens and I don't beat myself up when I have relapsed. In those times, reaching out to the community has always provided me with love and motivation. When one person is struggling, everyone comes together to help lift that person up.

I am now very strong in my sobriety and know with all my heart, I won't ever go back to hell. The tools and support from QS, the daily blogs from Jo and the gentle encouragement and being part of something special has been wonderful in my recovery. A constant source of motivation, inspiration and support. I dread to think where I would be if I hadn't found QS and I cannot thank you all enough."

Elvira, UK

"I joined QS at the end of last summer, after having spent four weeks and a lot of money, on a rehab programme. What I wasn't told was that the programme involved doing the steps and sitting in rooms for ever after 'sharing'. That works for a lot of people but it just didn't work for me. I'd tried it before and , being a quiet, private person, just sitting there trying to think of something to say was just awful. That just isn't me - so after the rehab I was totally depressed and desolate thinking that if that didn't work , with all that money spent, then what on earth would.

Then I stumbled upon Jo De Rosa and QS - what a revelation. A totally different way of thinking ! She said that I am not stuck in addiction - that with the right tools I can free myself from the treadmill of addiction and live a drug free life - after all she'd done it herself. This programme is not just about giving up your substance of addiction but embracing a totally new way of life through a discipline of living, essentially meditation and other practices which Jo makes enjoyable and not just a chore through her daily inspirational blogs.

After decades of negative brainwashing I am now beginning to have hope - there is never really a magic wand but with all the practical advice and inspiration Jo gives there is at last the chance to live our lives as if we had never been addicted in the first place. It takes work ... but ... wow ... is it worth it!"

Lisa, UK
"Thank you Jo for birthing QS and creating a safe secure place for everyone to discover themselves, find the courage to speak their truth and embrace self-love. Meditation has changed my life in such an unexpected way and shown me there is a way to freedom from addiction.
You truly are a modern day Angel."

C, Thailand
"Thank you so much for being a beacon of hope to so many people and offering your wisdom and transformative tools in such a down-to-earth accessible way."

Joy, UK
"I joined QS because I am a food addict. I would previously not have aligned myself with a programme for other addictions. I just completed my first year, and I have never felt out of place. In fact, I have always been supported with far more empathy than the majority of food related programmes I have been involved with and there are many. I believe in that the 12 Steps are a great foundation, but I cannot believe that repeating constantly that I am food addict is not helpful and reinforces where I don't want to be.

When I first met Jo I talked to her about my sugar addiction and the cravings I experienced she acknowledged of how difficult it was for food addicts as other addicts could stop using and food addicts couldn't. The first year has give me a great start and given me the willingness to look at things I would never have dared to before. I can't wait to see what Jo has in store for year 2."

Elle, UK

"Things had got very black for me again after a third unsuccessful attempt at alternative recovery programmes. My drinking and drugging was making me, and everyone around me miserable, and problems were piling up. I joined QS with both reservation and anticipation with a side order of hope!

I didn't start daily meditation, though I had been doing a bit, until after my wonderful week-long retreat in Suffolk at QS HQ. The retreat really lit the fire in my rocket, which propelled me to where I am today, feeling free. The struggle with substances has left me and although I slipped a few times in the early days, I found a wonderful supportive community and tools to get me straight back on track. I'm a completely different person, I love myself, I love my life and I am immensely grateful that I found this lifeline of a course!

Ps. It's more of a 'way of life' than a course!"

Comments From The Private Forum

K, Online Member
"Been feeling cravings in the past few days. I just walked to the shop and the craving was like a mist. It was a mist of memories surrounding me.

It felt like a lot of occasions on a dark, autumn night, going to the shop with the intention of buying booze. However this time that was not the intention. I was just buying provisions for our dinner.

I remembered how it felt to be going to the shop to satisfy a craving, and later to buy more. I remembered the hell I felt in when waking the next day, I would have to go for a walk in the dark morning air to deal with my anxiety and panic.

These cravings aren't serious. I know I will get to a year, which is 13/12/17. I have not meditated every day like I committed to in December 2016. I have not felt the need. I have been a lot more mindful and changed a lot. I am a different person. A changed for my better person.
I think the need is all too clear now. Meditating is the key to getting beyond 12 months sober. I know it."

L, Residential Retreat and Online Member
"Three months of beauty, love, and awe …I awoke to this sunrise the other week, three months into my new life in sobriety, and felt utter awe at the beauty, as though someone had painted love with brushstrokes across the sky. It took my breath away. And like me today, this photo is not altered in any way (for poetic licence, let's forget my roll-up addiction) – it is the natural beauty of source. It IS.

This programme has never been about alcohol for me, although I needed the tools to free myself from that addiction (arse on cushion, guys, every time!), it is a programme for living my best life, for a way of being in the world, for spiritual growth, for love, beauty, truth – the conditions to come home to my essence self and it has blown my heart wide open and replaced an empty, black void with abundant light and love.

I AM SO loved-up I could pee my pants with excitement. I have been a long time follower of Mooji and now have a list of spiritual teachers (Dyer, Braden, Massaro) to delve into and enhance my spiritual connection. The bridge to this life, meditation, as it embraces the silence within us and our conscious contact with source.
Hallelujah Jazz Hands!!

I am steadfast in my new life -all thoughts have energy and I try my best today to have empowering, rather than disempowering ones.

I am here because of the choices I have made. The choice to drink and now the choice not to drink. It takes action. Today I merge with the NOW. I have warmth and shelter and love and hope.

My partner has come back to me, my family want to hear from me today and I am so deeply blissful and happy – after THREE MONTHS. And I am kind today. I live with an attitude of giving, rather than ego and me me me, let's not forget about ME! Poor me. Actually, I find the false self (ego) easier to manage when living from the heart and looking to serve, rather than filling my boots with self-serving ego. The heart holds such startling intelligence.

When drunk, I used to phone up the vet and ask him to come out and put me down. This still makes me laugh today – I did this on countless occasions. It's a great party story. Yet today I wonder what that must have felt like to him. It must have been distressing – he sent me out pet bereavement counselling literature because he just didn't know what to do. I feel sad about that, even though I am laughing as I type. Perhaps there is a letter in my heart waiting to be written to him.

The world holds much beauty and peace and that is what I will be manifesting too. Lovers of humanity embrace all, including the dark, yet today I choose to live in the light and SHINE, with red-hot passion."

L, Residential Retreat and Online Member

"Last weekend my partner was drinking fizz and I was aware of two things: firstly, I was genuinely glad I did not want alcohol in my body and I felt a bit sorry for those who believe it enhances life! Secondly, he threw away what he didn't want to drink and I thought what an odd thing to do. Why not drink it all!! Laughing here – 'normal' drinkers are a strange breed!! My sister also wanted to put white wine in a risotto and although I knew it would be cooked off, I asked her to leave it out all together. Today, the thought of alcohol in my system is abhorrent. It has no hold for me other than repulsion – who knew!! I used to scoff that shit."

E, Online Member

"Thanks Jo. I'm spending a lot of time thinking about my core values. I've always felt a bit all over the place, as though I'm not truly living as me and always in some sort of internal conflict. I'm having to go quite deep to ask big and quite difficult questions about what my values really are. I'm also realising that it is only through sobriety that I can even ask these questions, never mind hear some of the answers and then dare to act on them! xx"

E, Online Member
"A quick message to say how excited I am about the upcoming tour. I absolutely love the idea of local, monthly meetings and just let me know if I can help with anything at all. I am only in week 9 but your guided meditations and the group support have been utterly transformational. Unlike my previous AF period which was dominated by the fear of what might happen if and when I ever had another drink, this AF period is dominated by the feeling of unbounded freedom and the joy of finally feeling at home in myself and the world. Thank you so much for opening up the world to me again xx"

V, Online Member
"As I walked home last night i reflected on how much i have changed. I thought about and imagined drinking wine and it just felt like empty spacy depression. And meditation keeps showing me what I need to work on.... But its all good. Glad i ripped the Band Aid off."

J, Residential Retreat and Online Member
"I came here hopeful, yet characteristically sceptical. Since being here, in just five days I've learnt a powerful new perspective about our ability to change and learnt things about myself at different levels; emotionally, cognitively and relationally that have helped me to understand myself better. I have genuinely experienced the effects of

the ideas on which QS is based, e.g; quantum moments which have validated the ideas. I have loved getting to know, support and receive genuine care and support from the people I have met here."

S, Residential Retreat and Online Member
"Love my QS family"

C, Residential Retreat and Online Member
"This has been a beautiful and revealing experience for me. The combination of scientific information, spiritual experiences and healing therapies have shifted me into a different place. It is lighter, airier, with new possibilities – ones I hadn't dreamed of. It's exciting! The course was delivered with great care and love.
If you want to change your life and be free of the struggle, misery and slavery of addiction, or ingrained negative thinking patterns and behaviours, then pack your bag, open your mind and walk towards this door. Push it open and find the magic. It's there when you're ready."

M, Online Member
"Having major shifts now, becoming lighter the more time I spend in meditation. The quantum downloads that Jo and many of you have posted about are finally happening to me!! Have not had wine in 22 days, I drank the day before we evacuated for the hurricane to help ease my anxiety. I really shouldn't have as alcohol and now I've discovered sugar in general cause me to get very emotional, I get a rush for a very short period of time and then crash. I can't do the roller coaster anymore. I'm observing my emotions, actually feeling them instead of

reacting to them has made me realize that It's time to give it up. Focused on removing sugar from my diet 100%. I have also been drinking 3 L of water daily and juicing. Committed to drinking 2 green juices a day, made at home"

T, Residential Retreat and Online Member
"I love this community. It's the pot of gold at the bottom of the rainbow!"
Namaste

E, Residential Retreat and Online Member
"I completely agree that sober doesn't equal boring I am having so much fun !
I'm keeping the word no tho! No has become empowering for me actually as I have said yes too many times.
NO I won't come to the boozy party even tho you are a close friend
NO I don't want a alcoholic drink, sugary cake, caffeinated drink
NO I can't help out on this occasion even tho I feel obliged to as I have too much on.
NO treating me like that is not acceptable and
NO I am not going to conform to societal norms
Xxx"

T, Residential Retreat and Online Member
"It really works, it really can happen to you. Jo told me at the beginning of my journey to believe all or nothing. And so I did and have through the ups and downs. Recently last week I've suddenly noticed change and shifts happening. After many hours of focus I'm able

to sit, straight back in mediation for longer without pain. Way pass my goal!

I've just realised some yoga stretches and flexes that I couldn't even start when I started I'm now fully doing. I'm starting to move out of recovery and into fun. Letting go more with conscious positive thinking. Not trying so hard!!

There's more beauty in the things I'm doing. I still have areas to work on no doubt and things to achieve but I want to tell any one struggling – it's actually happening! Layers of pain do fade with commitment in time!
Believe
List of words to cut out of your life:
Can't
No
Won't
Maybe
Hate
Problems
Excuse
Sorry
Don't
Shouldn't
Blessings and have a wonderful day!"

S, Residential Retreat and Online Member
"I've always loved your lanes blog Jo, because whatever I am working on and wherever I am, every time I drive on a dual carriageway or motorway I'm reminded of where I'm at with what I'm doing and if I'm dancing between lanes I commit pretty pronto to one or the other."

R, Online Member

"I did it!

I came to Ireland for a crazy music industry media wedding awash with free booze and plentiful drugs and I remained sober!

I danced, I ate, I laughed!

I ran along the beach.

I remember everything.

Including that I can't really dance but I love it.

I'm so grateful and I Am proud of myself.

Off for a hotel breakfast.

Sending love and thanks to the quantum, the group and jo.

Have a peaceful happy day

Xxx"

N, Residential Retreat and Online Member

"You have all helped me to make feel strong enough to take my life back..

Can't thank you all enough xx"

G, Residential Retreat and Online Member

"For me, the retreat was a drawing a line in the sand and I had to abide by that decision and take it forward to the new reality. I couldn't have done this without the total immersion of the retreat."

L, Residential Retreat and Online Member

"Today I realized that my sobriety is my real identity. I can honestly say that this has been the most beautiful year. Realization of really knowing my heart and getting to know myself better. It's 8 months this Monday, can't quite believe it. Xxx"

S, Online Member
"Morning beautiful tribe, I'm all for adding to the toolkit to help sobriety.
Being here has to be the biggest, the support, love and understanding is just unique and I feel blessed everyday I found QS."

S, Residential Retreat and Online Member
"You really do have the BEST of times sober. You reach a point with booze (my ex addiction) where there is NO fun to be had in a bottle. It would take a lot to convince me now that there ever was. For me, over time, it became hideously isolating rather than 'social'. If you're not quite there yet, stick with it and do the work (meditation) because freedom is amazing! Believe that you can do it, because you can. You deserve it because you are worth it"

D, Residential Retreat and Online Member
"I agree about meditation and want to tell newbies that mine is sometimes still rubbish, after 16 months in this programme. But sometimes great and always essential. Ultimately rewarding... it's giving you invisible superpowers (to calm yourself when you hit stress or triggers), so keep doing it. Find lots of different ones: short, long, with music, guided, or live group meditations in your community"

E, Online Member
"I am so grateful for finding Jo and QS. It's nearly the end of my first year and I have struggled horribly at times feeling that nothing works for me. Even since I've been sober it seems to have been physically but not mentally – a constant struggle.

I have decided that I need to live alone as my home circumstances aren't conducive to being calm and having lasting sobriety. But looking back over this past year I can see how things have changed and how I have changed – made me stronger and more able to live life on my terms. I hope this doesn't sound depressing – it's all good stuff – just me metamorphosing into the butterfly I was meant to be – at last. xxx"

D, Residential Retreat and Online Member

"I have had breast cancer. I have numbed out and made my life and my daughter's life very difficult by drinking too much, shouting at her, flying into a sudden rage, staying in crisis mode in my mind and allowing anger, frustration and ultimately fear to run the show. Now I don't have to do that anymore. I can turn on the happy hormones and let my body know it is safe. It really is a question of choosing our thoughts. Hallelujah!"

N, Residential Retreat and Online Member

"It's the best thing I ever did (the residential retreat). Changed my life. We're all on a journey and to be honest it's nothing but a magical one. I see that now after 8 months sober. If we didn't have this problem or gift we wouldn't be the colourful souls that we are. Keep strong and take it all in!"

S, Residential Retreat and Online Member

"Today it is exactly 1 year since I went on residential retreat at Jo's and more than a year since I found sobriety from booze. Looking back to who and what I was a year ago is to be frank astonishing. I was so unhappy and unable to find my way out of where I was at. I was such a victim. At the end of the retreat I experienced my first ever gong wash and at the time said it made me feel like I had been reborn. Little did I know then how accurate a description that was! Shortly after my retreat, I trusted in the quantum, followed my heart and jumped. My life is totally different now. I am future me and she is me. I am so happy and ready for the next level of whatever the quantum holds for me."

L, Online Member
"Living my dream Jo
I simply love being sober x"

E, Online Member
"Nearly 10 months alcohol free and I have realised the depression has gone. Don't need Prozac any more."

T, Online Member
"I love the total change in mindset when I go away now! I seek to find the best meditation spot or yoga site instead of the best pub. I'm looking for peace rather than hectic, I'm grateful for my surroundings rather than taking them for granted, I'm happy in each moment rather than seeking something else!! Namaste X"

J, Online Member
"Very profound day.. This could never have been like this if I would have been drinking.. My reasons to not drink just get deeper and filled with more gratitude the more time goes on. Love it"

M, Residential Retreat and Online Member
"My meditation practise has changed so much since joining QS. As soon as I sit and close my eyes I am plugged in. It's not always easy, but those sweet spots are sure worth it. Thank you Jo De Rosa"

J, Online Member
"I feel hungover today. I had a very sociable evening of spontaneous fun and a very late night. It was fab though, absolutely fab.
Its now like I have a new gift and it's a gift of being drunk at the best stage, without ANY alcohol.
Gone are any feelings of missing out on anything.
Gone are any associations with alcohol for anything…"

V, Online Member
"I had a burst of sheer joy in sobriety this morning and that is something i could not imagine 18 months ago!"

J, Online Member
"Oh wow, I did it. ONE YEAR TODAY WITHOUT ANY ALCOHOL. Not one drop. Omg, what an eye opening year it's been. Being alcohol free has shown me so much.
Now I am like how I was before I had ever experienced a drink.

I no longer associate alcohol with fun or think it relaxes me. I have un-wired all those firing brain neurons.
It has been quite sad at times though in that it has changed my relationships with others. (not everybody)
Many people have fallen out of my life, but I ain't here to please others or change myself to fit in. I am here to be my authentic self and be brave enough to live it, which is

why I quit in the first place, it was numbing me.

I actually still enjoy being around people who are having a good old drink. It's fun, it's funny and it reminds me of that stage of feeling tipsy, which I loved at the time.. I just leave at the point where they start telling me the same thing 25 times. I did that plenty of times myself, so no judgement either.

I could never ever have achieved and be doing what I am doing now if I was still drinking and I am.not talking serious drinking either, just regular weekend binge drinking of 2/3 bottles of wine all in all and maybe a couple of glasses in the week.

I now know the meaning of alcohol being a depressant. I used to think that meant if you are depressed then alcohol makes it worse. I didn't think that applied to me. Omg, now I know differently.

On a scale of 1/10 As a regular wine drinker I would score my general daily mood as a 7. After about 7/8 weeks of no alcohol that score went up to a 9. I felt amazing and high on life itself.
This has now become my new normal and I don't want to give that up or all the other health benefits I have experienced alongside it.

I don't want congratulating. I want anyone who reads this to be inspired to live the fullest version of their happiest, most authentic self however that is to you.
If it's one thing I have learnt from not wasting so much time hungover, it's that hangovers last longer than we think they do.

We are not here for long, time passes very quickly and the only time we have is now.
The most important thing in life is to be happy with WHO you are, how you live and to share that vibe with others."

J, Online Member
"I struggled too this week
For those who don't know, I am just about a year sober. When you are struggling you need to go below the surface and ask what it is you REALLY need, because I promise you it's not the drink, it's something else..
In the early days, there are a few brain neurons that need un wiring and Trigger meditation is your first key. Please do it no matter what. It's a very powerful meditation and you don't need to know the how it works, you just need to do it and it's always there to go back to."

References

Papers:
Paulson, S., Davidson, R. J., Jha, A., & Kabat-Zinn, J. (2013). Becoming conscious: the science of mindfulness. *Annals of the New York Academy of Sciences, 1303,* 87–104. doi:10.1111/nyas.12203. PMCID: Policy Exempt -- Not a peer-reviewed research article

Davidson, R. J., & Lutz, A. (2008). Buddha's brain: Neuroplasticity and meditation. *IEEE Signal Processing Magazine, 25*(1), 171-174. PMCID: PMC2944261

Dahl, C. J., Lutz, A., & Davidson, R. J. (2015). Reconstructing and deconstructing the self: Cognitive mechanisms in meditation practice. *Trends in Cognitive Sciences, 19*(9), 515–23. PMCID: PMC4595910

Books:
Goleman, Daniel-Narrator, and Dalai Lama. *Destructive Emotions.* New York, New York: Bantam Dell, 2003. Print.

Account of the Mind and Life Institute meetings with HH Dalai Lama: March 2000

Pert, PH.D, Candace B. *Molecules of Emotion.* USA. Scribner, 1997. Print

Dispenza, Joe. *Breaking The Habit Of Being Yourself.* Carlsbad, Calif.: Hay House, 2012. Print.

Dispenza, Joe. *You Are The Placebo.* Hay House, 2014. Print.

A combination of quantum physics, neuroscience, brain chemistry, biology and genetics explaining in detail how you can rewire your brain

Ricard, Matthieu, and Xuan Thuan Trinh. *The Quantum And The Lotus*. New York: Crown Publishers, 2001. Print.

A Buddhist monk and a professor of astronomy discuss the many remarkable connections between the teachings of Buddhism and findings of recent science.

His Holiness the Dalai Lama,. *The Universe In A Single Atom*. New York: Morgan Road Books, 2005. Print.

The Dalai Lama has a lifelong interest in scientific study and religious practice, making astonishing connections between the two worlds.

Other:
What The Bleep Do We Know. 2006. DVD.

A film about quantum physics and neuroscience that initially sparked my interest in the subject in 2007.

Dialogues with the Dalai Lama – Mind and Life Institute. 2016. [ONLINE] Available at: https://www.mindandlife. org/mind-and-life-dialogues/

Links to yearly meetings between the Mind and Life Institute and HH Dalai Lama, talking about the bridge between science and spirituality. Videos available from 1987 to present day.

Online Links For Further Reading About Time:
Time's Arrow: an unsolved general physics question about the direction of time. See www.wikipedia.org/wiki/arrow_of_time [ONLINE]

Times' Arrow. See https://www.wired.com/2016/09/arrow-of-time/ [ONLINE]

Einstein's belief that the separation between past, present, and future is only an illusion. See http://everythingforever.com/einstein.htm [ONLINE]

Einstein's take on Relativistic Time. See http://www.exactlywhatistime.com/physics-of-time/relativistic-time/ [ONLINE]

The philosophy of time. See http://www.exactlywhatistime.com/philosophy-of-time/modern-philosophy/ [ONLINE]

Online Links For Further Reading About Food:
Studies on the benefits of an alkaline diet. See https://www.ncbi.nlm.nih.gov/pmc/articles/PMC3195546/ [ONLINE]

The fat and sugar conversation; which one makes you fat? See http://uk.businessinsider.com/eating-fat-wont-make-you-fat-gain-weight-says-doctor-2017-11 [ONLINE]

Why fat doesn't make you fat. See https://www. huffingtonpost.com/elizabeth-rider/fat-doesnt-make-you-fat-b_b_8078620.html [ONLINE]

The problem with gluten. See https://paleoleap.com/11-ways-gluten-and-wheat-can-damage-your-health/ [ONLINE]

About Us – Our Programmes

UK Based

Inner Guidance Retreat Centre is our home and where we run our UK workshops and retreats. Set in stunning country scenery in the East of England our 500-year-old Tudor house has bags of charm and history. You couldn't find a better spot for a day, weekend or whole week of metamorphosis.

Choose from a one-day workshop or in-depth five-day retreat and enjoy Dom's amazing clean-cooking and Jo's transformational offerings.

Online Programme

And if you can't get to the UK then the Quantum Sobriety online programme has members from all over the world, meaning there is support at all times of day from the community. On joining you receive your first meditation, a video from Jo and access to the private forum. Then once a month Jo, or one of her team, holds a live webinar and weekly livestream trainings where you can ask questions about your journey directly.

Meditations

If you would like similar meditations to the ones contained in this book without the commitment of the online programme, you'll find 'The Quantum Series' which have been recorded by Jo and are available to download on the Quantum Superpowers website.

Book

Thank you for reading this book and I truly hope that it has created a shift in your perspective of addiction and how powerful your mind really is. Please pass it on to someone who you think may also benefit, or keep your copy and buy them their own (I love to make notes in books that inspire me, and they then stay in my private book collection and not in our public library).

Don't forget that we would love to know the results of your Beginning and End Questionnaires; you can add your answers into our (private and secure) online survey and help us get this approach to the people that need it: www.quantumsobriety.com/workbook

Get in contact with us here:

www.QuantumSobriety.com
info@QuantumSobriety.com

www.InnerGuidance.co.uk
info@InnerGuidance.co.uk

www.QuantumSuperpowers.com
info@QuantumSuperpowers.com

Inner Guidance Retreat Centre is available to rent and a whole range of different teachers bring groups to the house all year round. The Quantum Sobriety five day retreats are held monthly and the one day workshops periodically through the year. Check the website for current details, dates, prices and availability.

Other Titles By Jo De Rosa

If You Could Have Anything... What Would It Be?